TABLE OF CONTENTS

INTRODUCTION TO THE PUBLICATION

Problem Solving – A Basic Mathematics Goal is a two-part publication designed as an in-service tool for teachers of grades K-9. Goals for this publication are: to help teachers to become better mathematical problem solvers, to introduce techniques and materials helpful in improving student problem solving abilities, and to suggest ways to organize the curriculum and daily instruction to achieve problem solving goals.

Becoming A Better Problem Solver is the introductory booklet of the publication. It is based upon the postulate that a teacher should become a better problem solver in order to teach problem solving more effectively to students. The booklet provides an overview of problem solving as a process used daily by all individuals and as a curriculum goal important to all disciplines. A substantial portion of the booklet is devoted to introducing *strategies,* methods useful in getting started on problems and successfully solving them. Though the booklet uses mathematical problems as the medium for problem solving discussions and activities, the techniques have application to virtually any problem area.

The second booklet of this publication concerns the teaching and curriculum aspects of problem solving. **A Resource for Problem Solving** is a digest of selected topics integral to successful problem solving instruction. Arranged in a topical format of associated ideas, sections are written for independent teacher use. These sections may be studied sequentially or referred to singly, as needed. Section titles for booklet two are:

TEACHING	*CURRICULUM*
Introduction to Teaching Problem Solving	*Getting Started*
Research and Psychological Summaries	*Primary Instruction*
Looking Back Strategies	*Intermediate and Junior High Instruction*
Teaching Considerations	*Creating a Problem Solving Environment*
Choosing Different Teaching Modes	*Organizing the Curriculum*
Story Problems and Number Sentences	*Calculators in Problem Solving*
	Problem List
	Bibliography and Selected References

This two-part publication entails a recognition of and commitment to problem solving as a fundamental goal of education which is within reach of every student. Though problem solving skills are generally recognized as important attributes of the educated person, past development of these skills has been more the product of chance and individual effort than well-defined curriculum planning. This publication is an attempt to provide definition and direction to teaching efforts to achieve problem solving outcomes in one curriculum area – mathematics – but with easily discernible bridges to other subjects.

ABOUT THIS BOOKLET

Problem solving is something you learn about and become more skillful with by actually doing. There is a limit to that which you can acquire by reading about or observing how a problem is solved by someone else. Therefore, this booklet is intended for **interactive use** by you. Occasionally, you will be asked to analyze your own thinking in order to define more clearly your attitudes about a problem solving topic. Sometimes you will be a spectator, reading along and observing how a particular technique is useful in solving a seemingly difficult problem. At other times, you will be invited "down out of the stands" to participate actively, to stop reading, to solve another "seemingly difficult" problem. You will be challenged to use strategies about which you have been reading. Then **you** will be the one making the decisions, guiding the problem attack, experiencing the discoveries, and reaping the satisfaction of solving the problem.

This booklet is planned in sections which are preceded by objectives for that section. The first section is an introduction to problem solving. Activities associated with this section are important as benchmarks of your attitudes and beliefs about problem solving. Your responses will serve as reference points for subsequent extensions of your understanding of problem solving.

The major portion of this booklet uses a strategies approach to problem solving. Sections are organized by clusters of related problem solving strategies. Each strategy of a cluster is discussed and illustrated in the solution of a problem. You are than asked to solve one or two problems using the same strategy. Hints and follow-up discussions accompany each problem. After the introduction of three to five strategies, a set of challenge problems follows which can be solved by using one or more of the strategies studied in that section. Hints for solving these problems are found in Appendix A. Solutions for the problems are given in Appendix B.

The strategies discussed in this booklet are appropriate for introduction in grades 3-9. Problems which you are asked to solve carry a grade level designation. This indicator should enable you to begin to reflect upon the kinds of problems which can and should be introduced at various grade levels. Furthermore, we hope that you will use the example and challenge problems as resources for your work with students.

This booklet may be studied individually or be used by groups of teachers. However used, we recommend that the booklet be studied in sections. There is enough substance in each section to warrant consideration, reflection, and perhaps even classroom experimentation before starting a new section. Use of the booklet in this prescribed way will require six lessons or individual meetings.

The advantage of group work is that individuals may interact and stimulate each other to achieve additional insights. Members of a group may take turns acting as the group facilitator, guiding conversation and keeping activities moving. Use of a resource person to assist group study is a matter for local decision. We do strongly recommend that a variety of concrete materials be readily available for group or individual use in solving problems. See appendix C for a recommended list of such materials.

This booklet *can* help you become more aware of generally productive techniques to employ in solving problems. It *can* induce you to reflect on a problem after its solution, focusing on the more important process aspects of the solution rather than the answer. But it *cannot* make you a better problem solver through reading alone. The key to successful use of these materials and to your becoming a better problem solver is your *willingness to solve* as many problems as possible through its use.

AN OVERVIEW OF PROBLEM SOLVING

As a result of studying this section, you will be able to:

- *discuss the role of problem solving as an activity in daily life;*
- *identify alternative views of problem solving as an educational activity;*
- *specify the difference between a problem and an exercise or task;*
- *state the characteristics of a problem solving strategy.*

A Tale of Two Students

Episode: A fifth grade student working on an assignment, gets up from her desk, walks over to the mathematics resource corner and selects cubes from a variety of other materials. She returns to her desk and begins arranging the small cubes, stopping occasionally to write something in a table that she has sketched on her paper. Then she turns back to organizing the blocks into a different arrangement. The girl is moving purposefully, confidently, and obviously is enjoying the activity. Other student activities are occurring near her but she is unmindful. She is totally engrossed in her own efforts. Now she pauses momentarily to look at her table and suddenly bursts forth with, "I got it! I got it!"

Episode: Elsewhere in another classroom in the same school, a sixth grade student is tapping her pencil on the desk, looking back and forth at her book and paper, occasionally starting to jot something down, but quickly crossing it out. The girl frowns frequently, appears bored, and acts somewhat frustrated by this activity. Now staring around the room, the girl takes one last look at her book and then slaps down her pencil with a disgusted, "I can't **do** this stuff!"

Two children of equal intelligence and similar backgrounds engaged in problem solving in their respective mathematics classes. One child, flushed with excitement, exudes pride, satisfaction, self-accomplishment, and positive self-image. The other child is frustrated and troubled, has voiced her failure, and is filled with self-doubt, dissatisfaction, and negative feelings about herself and her capacity to be successful at this activity.

Why is one child a successful problem solver and the other frustrated by the same experience? There is no simple answer to this question. Each child is a product of many prior experiences that impinge upon this particular learning situation. Her interests, motivation, skills, and a whole range of other factors may be important contributors to her success or failure at solving particular problems.

Yet in looking back at the two situations, we can note one subtle distinction between the actions of the two students. Both are addressing a situation they have not faced before. Something is asked of each student that requires her to overcome some obstacle. Both students have met that blockage. However, the first student is doing something productive. She is moving purposefully toward overcoming or removing the obstacle. She has selected manipulative materials to aid her and goes about her task in an organized manner. She records her findings in a table. In a short time, she achieves the breakthrough with the exhuberant, "I got it!" The second student is stymied. Every brief attempt at progressing with the problem is quickly crossed out. Her efforts are random and disorganized. It is readily apparent that she does not have an effective way to begin.

As educators, we cannot guarantee that we can make successful problem solvers of every student. But we can assure that students learn to use productive procedures to attack problems – procedures which give them that very important first step that gets them started toward resolving the problem situation. The purpose of this booklet is to make you familiar with these procedures.

Problem Solving as a Daily Activity

Problem solving is an activity in which each of us engage all the time. It begins when we are confronted with a situation involving an obstruction between us and something we want. The problem can be large such as: "How can we deal with air pollution?" or small, "Now, where did I leave that needle?" Problems can be short-range, "How can I get into my locked house without a key?" or long-range, "How can the injured girl regain full use of her arm after the accident?" Problems can be well-defined and specific: "How many gallons of water are required to fill this 18-ft. diameter swimming pool to a depth of 3½ feet?" Or a problem can be general and poorly defined, "What can be done to curb urban blight?"

Problems are something which confront everybody, large or small, young or old, rich or poor, every day. We sometimes even create problems to be resolved in the form of table games, athletic endeavors, puzzles, new situations, and new acquaintances. In short, solving problems is very much a part of everyday life, sometimes creating anxiety and frustration and hard work in their solution, but also being a source of relaxation, satisfaction, and mental stimulation.

Problem Solving in Education

As educators, we recognize the importance of problem solving and teach for its development in many different subjects and under several different labels. In science, we call it the discovery or inquiry approach. In social studies, we use case studies and role playing. In language arts, we talk of getting the main idea, comprehension, and word attack skills. In mathematics, we employ it in story problems, applications, and some discovery or skill building activities.

But teaching for problem solving means different things to different people. To some, it is any procedure that produces an answer. For these persons, the emphasis is on answer-getting. The process that one uses is incidental. The answer is the important outcome.

Others see problem solving as an activity wherein one practices a skill such as division with whole numbers. A problem presents a pseudo-realistic setting to motivate the student to apply the most recently studied skill in a simulated situation. We hope the student will gain the ability to transfer that skill to real situations. However, the central focus of such activities usually dwells on polishing or refining the specific skill.

Presenting a problem situation for which prerequisite skills have not yet been learned is another view of problem solving. It is a pedagogical approach in which one uses a problem situation to motivate the need for and to show the application of specific skills to be acquired. Skill development is emphasized but in the context of skills being important tools to achieve other goals.

Some view problem solving as a teachable process consisting of general techniques that can be applied to a large variety of dissimilar problems, problem settings, and subject matter. From this perspective, problem solving becomes an activity wherein the focus shifts to the thinking, techniques, and processes that one goes through to resolve a problem situation and produce an answer.

Activity I: Stop and take time to write down your present perceptions about problem solving in mathematics in five short declarative sentences beginning with: Problem solving . . .

Activity II: How much instructional time do you devote in your mathematics classes toward achieving problem solving objectives keyed to your Activity I responses?

File your responses to Activities I and II so that you can refer back to them periodically to determine whether your views change with continued study of these materials.

What is a Problem?

Newell and Simon [1977, p. 72] define a problem as a situation in which a person wants something and does not know immediately what series of actions he can perform to get it. In these materials, we are interested in mathematics problems. Therefore, an added dimension to our definition of a problem is that mathematical ideas be involved in the actions to resolve the situation.

Four elements are involved in our definition of a mathematical problem.

TO BE A MATHEMATICAL PROBLEM
• A situation must exist involving an initial state and a goal state. • The situation must involve mathematics. • A person must desire a solution (accept the problem). • There must be some blockage between the given and desired states.

For a situation to be a problem, it must be judged in relationship to an individual and a time. If a person is not interested in finding the prime numbers between 211 and 257, the situation is not a problem **for him**. Secondly, the individual must not know immediately how to proceed. The situation must be new to him, presenting some difficulty or obstacle which he must overcome.

If he has encountered this kind of situation before, then it may not present a problem to him now. But it was a problem when he first confronted it. Therefore, a problem for one person now may not be a problem for that person tomorrow. And it may not be a problem today for someone else. He either knows how to overcome the problem situation or does not care about the solution.

The distinction involving blockage is an important one because many persons confuse **a problem** with **an exercise** or **a task**. For example, if I ask you to find 387 x 469 you are confronted with an exercise. You know immediately how to proceed. You have faced similar tasks before.

We may desire a given goal state, and it may require time and effort to achieve. But unless one is presented with the perplexing difficulty of not knowing immediately how to proceed, he is not confronting a problem by our definition.

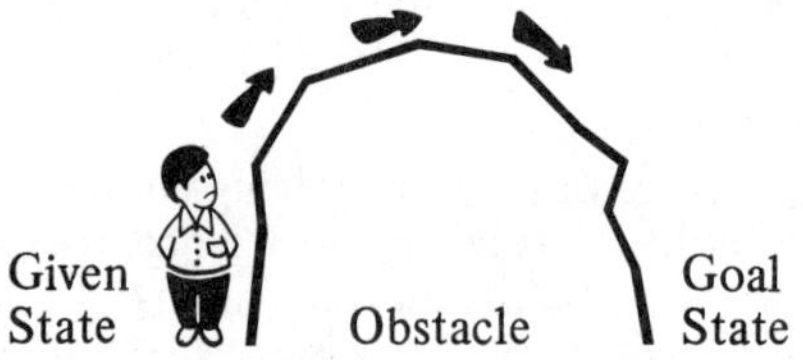

EXERCISE OR TASK

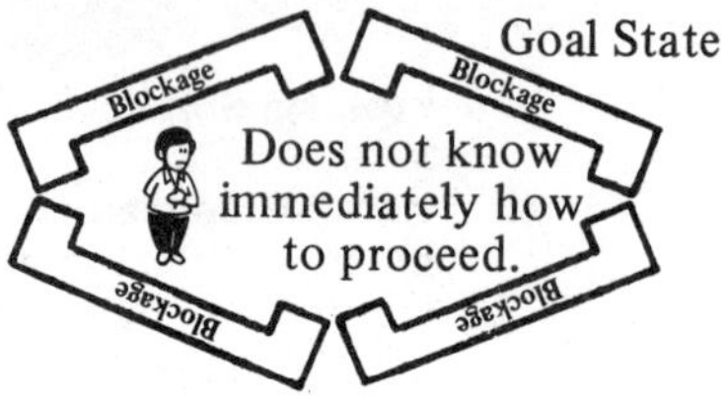

PROBLEM

Problem Solving

In problem solving, you must therefore expect to be challenged by situations you have not met previously, to be unsure about how to start, to be unaware of how much time or effort will be required for solution. Consequently, your attitude plays an important role. You must desire the solution goal to subject yourself to this kind of dilemma. You must have confidence that the obstacles are within your capability to overcome. You must believe that your thinking and problem solving skills are adequate to begin an attack upon the problem.

AFFECTIVE CONSIDERATIONS TO PROBLEM SOLVING
• You must desire the solution • You must feel that it is within your ability • You must believe that you can begin an attack on the problem.

Of these three considerations, the first two are easier to achieve. For the third to occur, you must have: (a) experience in solving problems; and (b) an understanding (explicit or intuitive) of general steps or procedures that are usually productive in solving problems. We call these general procedures, *strategies*.

PROBLEM SOLVING STRATEGIES
Look for a pattern Construct a table Account for all possibilities (systematically) Act it out Make a model Guess and check Work backwards Make a drawing, figure, or graph Select appropriate notation Restate the problem (in your own words) Identify wanted, given, and needed information Write an open sentence Identify a subgoal Solve a simpler (or similar) problem Change your point of view Check for hidden assumptions

Strategies are useful techniques for solving widely dissimilar problems of varying degrees of difficulty and complexity. They are actions which are not problem-specific. They represent procedures that you can use to make a problem clearer, simpler, smaller, or more manageable. Four important points associated with a strategies approach to problem solving are [Suydam, et al, p. 21]:

(a) strategies are general skills or abilities that can be learned;
(b) strategies are useful in a variety of problems;
(c) strategies may be used singly or in combinations to solve a single problem;
(d) strategies give the individual the tools with which to begin or continue productive work on a problem.

Many persons unconsciously make use of some or most of the strategies listed in the table above. However, they can become better problem solvers by becoming more aware of their use of specific strategies, developing others, and generally analyzing their thinking as they solve problems.

To become a better problem solver using the strategies approach, we recommend the following plan:

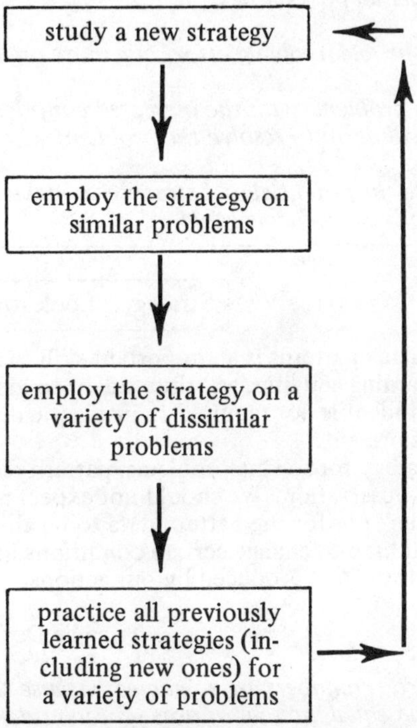

Using Strategies To Solve Problems

In this booklet, we shall study the previous list of strategies in clusters. Individual strategies will be discussed and illustrated in the solution of a problem. We will then ask you to solve another problem by employing that strategy. Hints and follow-up discussion will follow each of these problems. At the end of each cluster of strategies, a set of challenge problems will be presented to give you practice in selecting the correct strategy to apply to a problem.

Most good problems can be solved in a variety of ways. However, for the problems in the following sections to help you to grow in the strategies approach, we challenge you to employ the strategy or strategies of that section. Only solutions using these strategies will be given.

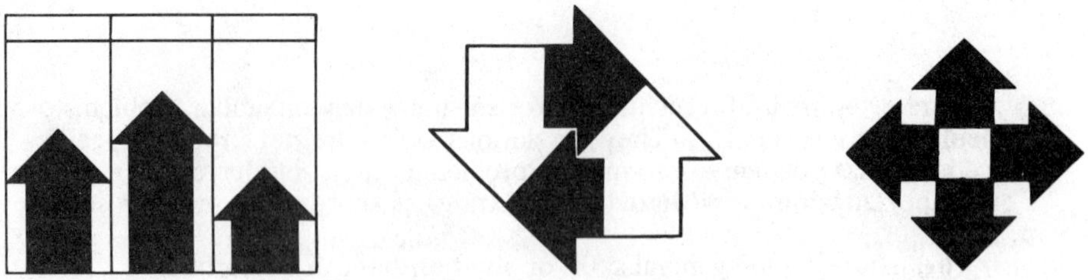

STRATEGIES–PART I

As a result of studying this section, you will be able to:

- *use three strategies in solving problems – look for a pattern, construct a table, consider all possibilities;*
- *initiate a problem solving effort in a more organized and systematic manner;*
- *approach problems with the increased confidence that you can determine an action that will begin to resolve the problem;*
- *appreciate the potential of a strategy to make a problem smaller, easier, and generally more manageable.*

Strategy: Look for a Pattern

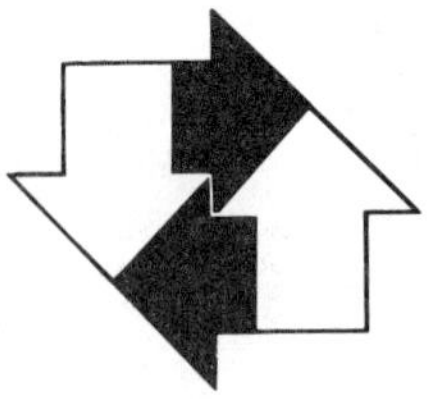

Recognizing patterns is an important skill that young students are encouraged to develop. Many early learning activities ask the student to identify a pattern for data presented to him. Usually, the student is not required to interact with the data except to identify and continue a pattern that is present.

As a strategy for solving problems, pattern recognition becomes more of an active search than a passive observation. We should not expect a pattern among problem data to automatically "jump out at us" nor for the pattern data to be already present and awaiting our inspection. We very likely will have to change certain conditions in the problem situation and *look for a pattern* to emerge by the effect produced by our actions.

Grades 3 & 4 Triangle Dot Numbers

Triangle dot numbers are so named because that number of dots can be used to form a triangle with an equal number of dots on each side.

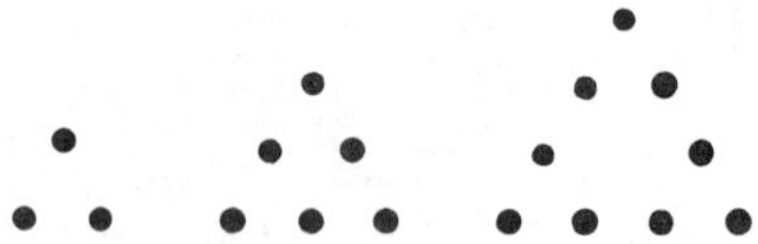

3 *6* *9*

triangle dot numbers

What triangle dot number has 10 dots on a side?

We could construct the triangle requested and count the dots. But we wish to practice the strategy *look for a pattern.* (After all, someone might ask us next about the triangle dot number for 200 dots on a side!)

Looking at our first three triangle dot numbers, we notice that three more dots are added each time as we progress from figure to figure.

If we compare dots on a side to groups of three dots we see:

Dots on a side:	2	3	4
Groups of three:	1	2	3

The number of groups of three is one less than the number of dots on a side. So! For 10 dots on a side, there must 9 groups of three. Our number is 27!

One way to improve your ability to find patterns is to look for other patterns in the same set of information. Where one pattern exists there are usually others close by.

Suppose we look for another pattern. Proceed around each triangle in one direction, circling the dots on each side that have not yet been circled and note the number.

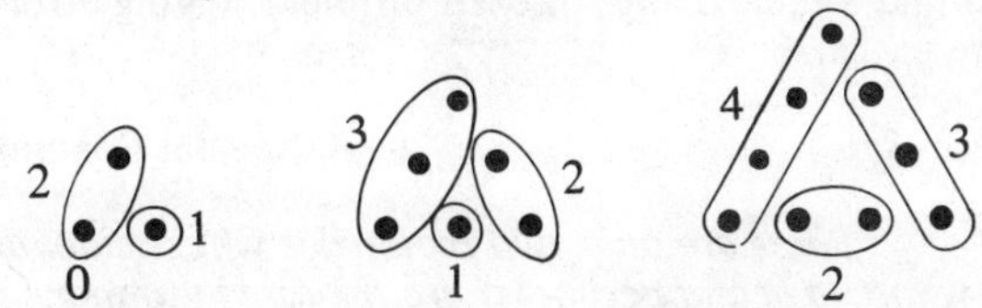

For each triangle, the pattern occurring is for the number of dots left on a side to decrease by one as we go around the triangle. So for a triangle with ten dots on a side, our circled groups would contain 10, 9, and 8 dots or 27 dots total.

You may have seen still another pattern for this problem.

Now it is your turn.

Grades 3 & 4 Pentagon Dot Numbers

Five, ten and fifteen are examples of pentagon dot numbers.

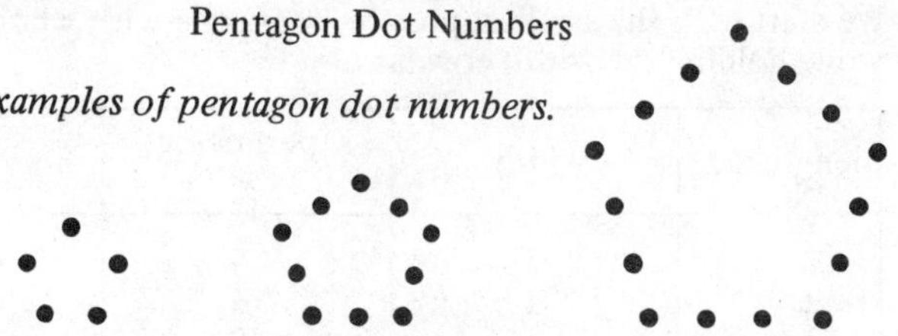

5 10 15

For the pentagon dot number 35, how many dots are on each side of its dot figure?

You are the problem solver this time. Remember to *look for a pattern.*

Stop reading and try to solve the problem.

If you kept on reading without working on the problem, you just broke confidence with these materials. You must work problems to learn more about problem solving. Now stop reading and work on the problem.

If you have not solved the problem, consider this hint: how do the number of dots on a side increase as the total number of dots increases? Now stop and work on the problem again.

The correct answer is 8 dots on a side. By looking at the number of dots on each side and comparing with the total, we have:

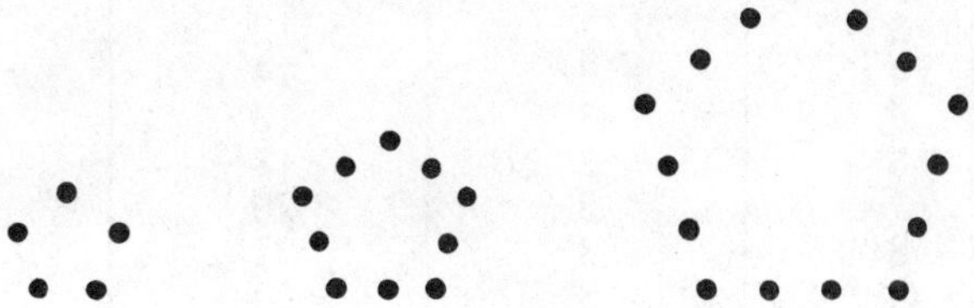

Dots per side:	2	3	4
Total number of dots:	5	10	15

We can see a pattern for the totals. They are multiples of five. Each total is the 5-multiple which is one less than the number of dots on a side for that figure. Since 35 = 7(5) the number of dots per side is **8**.

More important than the answer 8, however, is the fact that we can now answer more difficult questions such as *"How many dots are on each side of the pentagon dot figure for 195?"* **because we observed the pattern.**

Strategy: Construct a Table

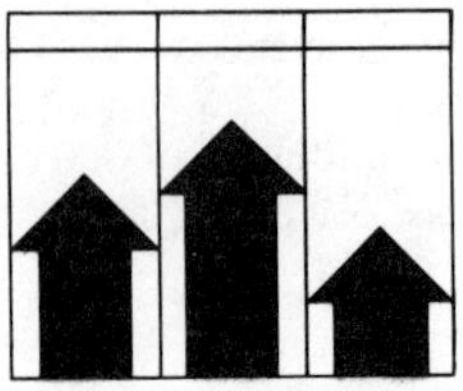

A strategy frequently used with *look for a pattern* is *construct a table.* By organizing data in tabular form, it is much easier to discover a pattern and to identify information which is missing. Because an appropriate table is an efficient means to classify and order a wealth of information, its use can free our thinking for other problem considerations. Equally important is the tangible record that a table makes of each problem solving effort so that we do not have to retrace unproductive paths.

Grades 5 & 6

Special Rectangles

There are only two rectangles whose sides are whole numbers and whose area and perimeter are the same number. What are they?

We have to draw upon certain background information. Area and perimeter of rectangles are involved so we must recall:

$$\text{area} = \text{length} \times \text{width} \quad \text{or} \quad A = l \times w$$
$$\text{perimeter} = 2(\text{length}) + 2(\text{width}) \quad \text{or} \quad p = 2l + 2w$$

Using a table with length, width, area and perimeter headings, we can organize our search. We start with the smallest possible rectangle with whole number dimensions and change the length while holding the width constant.

length	width	perimeter $2l + 2w$	area $l \times w$
1	1	4	1
2	1	6	2
3	1	8	3
4	1	10	4

By this point, we begin to notice a pattern in the perimeter and area columns that shows those values to be growing apart rather than coming closer together. Therefore, we abandon the search for rectangles with width 1 and continue with rectangles of width 2.

length	width	perimeter $2l + 2w$	area $l \times w$
2	2	8	4
3	2	10	6
4	2	12	8
5	2	14	10

Now the pattern indicates the perimeter and area values will continue to vary by the same amount, 4. So we continue on.

length	width	perimeter $2l + 2w$	area $l \times w$
3	3	12	9
4	3	14	12
5	3	16	15
* 6	3	18	18
7	3	20	21
8	3	22	24
9	3	24	27

We find one solution, $l = 6$ and $w = 3$. The perimeter-area pattern shows that further search with widths of 3 will be fruitless.

length	width	perimeter $2l + 2w$	area $l \times w$
4	4	16	16

Our very next try yields the second solution 4 by 4. Therefore, the only two rectangles whose sides are whole numbers and whose perimeters equal their area are 6 by 3 and 4 by 4. It is entirely another problem to show that 6 by 3 and 4 by 4 are the **only** solutions. But that is one we leave to the curious reader.

Making a table can sometimes be useful when a pattern is not involved, as this problem illustrates.

Grades 3 & 4 Horses to Ride

A riding stable owner has the following kinds of horses and ponies: Arabian mare, Apaloosa stallion, Palomino pony, Arabian pony, Palomino mare, Pinto stallion, Apaloosa mare, Palomino stallion, Pinto pony, and Arabian stallion. If he wants to have mounts of every size and breed combination, what types of horses or ponies should he obtain?

Stop reading and solve the problem by making a table.

By constructing the table according to horse size versus horse breed, we can enter the problem information and better determine what horses he has and the ones he needs.

Breed/Size	Stallion	Mare	Pony
Arabian	x	x	x
Apaloosa	x	x	
Palomino	x	x	x
Pinto	x		x

We can now easily see that the man needs an Apaloosa pony and a Pinto mare.

Strategy: Account for all Possibilities (systematically)

A third strategy sometimes used with *look for a pattern and construct a table* is *account for all possibilities.* This strategy does not mean that we have to examine all possibilities, but rather that we account for them in some systematic way. For example, you might be able to organize the possibilities into classifications. By using some selection criteria, you might dismiss some classes of possibilities before beginning a systematic search of the remaining possibilities. Recall that we used a systematic search earlier in the area-perimeter problem and were able to exclude certain categories of answers through the patterns we observed.

Consider the following problem.

Grades 5 & 6 Fertilizer Sale

You need 17 lb of fertilizer. What do you buy to obtain at least that amount at the lowest cost?

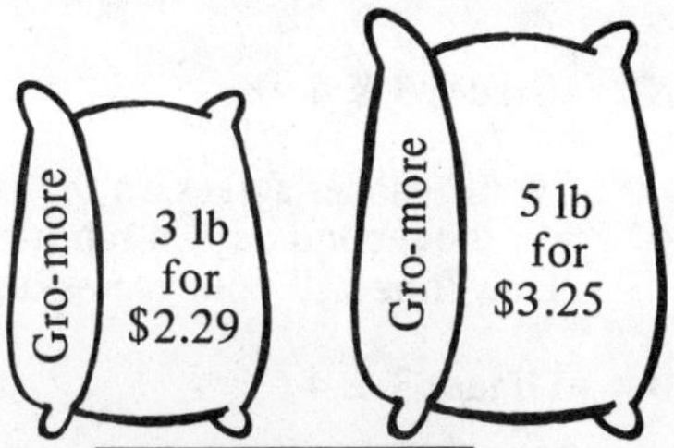

Fertilizer on Sale

To obtain the smallest amount equal or slightly exceeding 17 lb of fertilizer using 3-lb and 5-lb quantities, we can list these possibilities: four 5-lb bags; three 5-lb and one 3-lb bags; two 5-lb and three 3-lb bags; one 5-lb and four 3-lb bags; or six 3-lb bags.

Making a table to organize our possibilities, we can fill in the amount and determine a total cost for each fertilizer combination.

5-lb bags	Cost @ $3.25	3-lb bags	Cost @ $2.29	Total Amount	Total Cost	
4	$13.00			20 lb	$13.00	
3	$ 9.75	1	$ 2.29	18 lb	$12.04	*
2	$ 6.50	3	$ 6.87	19 lb	$13.37	
1	$ 3.25	4	$ 9.16	17 lb	$12.41	
		6	$13.74	18 lb	$13.74	

The *systematic accounting for all possibilities* and use of a table give us not only the cheapest combination to purchase – three 5-lb bags and one 3-lb bag at $12.04 – but also offer some interesting comparisons. It is cheaper to buy more than you need (18 lb for $12.04) than the exact quantity (17 lb for $12.41). The careful shopper ($12.04) can save $1.70 over the less attentive shopper ($13.74).

Try your hand at accounting for all possibilities on this problem.

Grades 3 & 4 An Astronautical Problem

The planet Klepton has only creatures with 3-legs (Triads) and 4-legs (Tetrads). Astronaut Janice could not bear to look at these ugly creatures. So she kept her eyes on the ground. On her first day on Klepton, she counted 31 legs. How many Triads and Tetrads did she meet?

Stop reading and work on the problem.

If you have not found the answers, go back and systematically consider how you can combine multiples of three and four to sum 31.

Our table shows the possibilities.

Tetrads (4 legs)	8	7	6	6	5	4	3	3	2	1	
Triads (3 legs)		1	2	3	4	5	6	7	8	9	10
Total Legs	32	31	30	33	32	31	30	33	32	31	30
Solution	No	Yes	No	No	No	Yes	No	No	No	Yes	No

Astronaut Janice might have met 8, 9, or 10 creatures!

So far, we have discussed the strategies one-by-one. But as we have already seen, they are frequently used in combinations. The following set of challenge problems can be solved by using one or more of the first three strategies. Hints for the problems are in Appendix A and solutions are in Appendix B.

Challenge Problems Set I

A. Grades 3 & 4 A Good Recess

Your teacher agrees on the first day of school to let you have 1 minute of recess, 2 minutes on the second day, 4 minutes on the third day, 8 minutes on the fourth day, and so on. How long will your recess be at the end of two weeks?

B. Grades 3 & 4 Growing Letters

(1) If the figure at the right is continued, how many letters will be in the M column?

(2) What column will contain 33 letters?

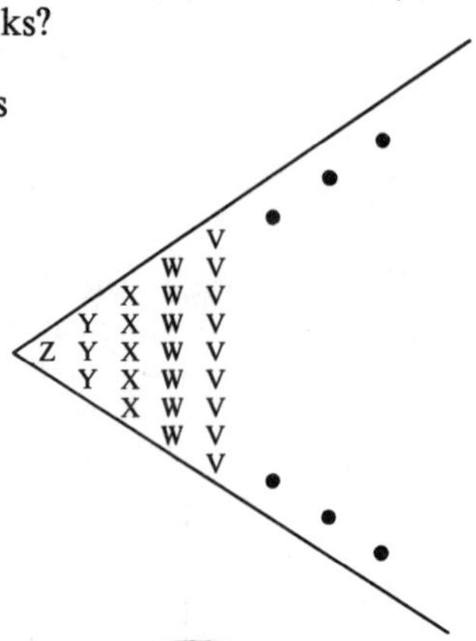

C. Any Grades Hands Together

When it is twelve o'clock, the hands on the clock face overlap. How many times will the hands again overlap as the clock runs until it is again twelve o'clock? (Count the second time it is twelve o'clock but not the first.)

D. Grades 5 & 6 — Odd Ways to 20

How many ways can you add 8 odd numbers to get a sum of 20? (You may use a number more than once.)

E. Grades 5 & 6 — My Checking Account

My bank has been charging me a monthly service charge of 25 cents plus 10 cents a check for my checking account. The bank now tells me it is changing to 50 cents a month service charge plus 8 cents a check and that this will save me money. How many checks must I write a month for this to be true?

Activity III: Choose any of the problems discussed so far which are labeled at or below the grade level you teach. Give the question to your class and ask them to work individually on the problem. Observe individuals carefully. What problem solving behaviors are similar? How do some individuals differ?

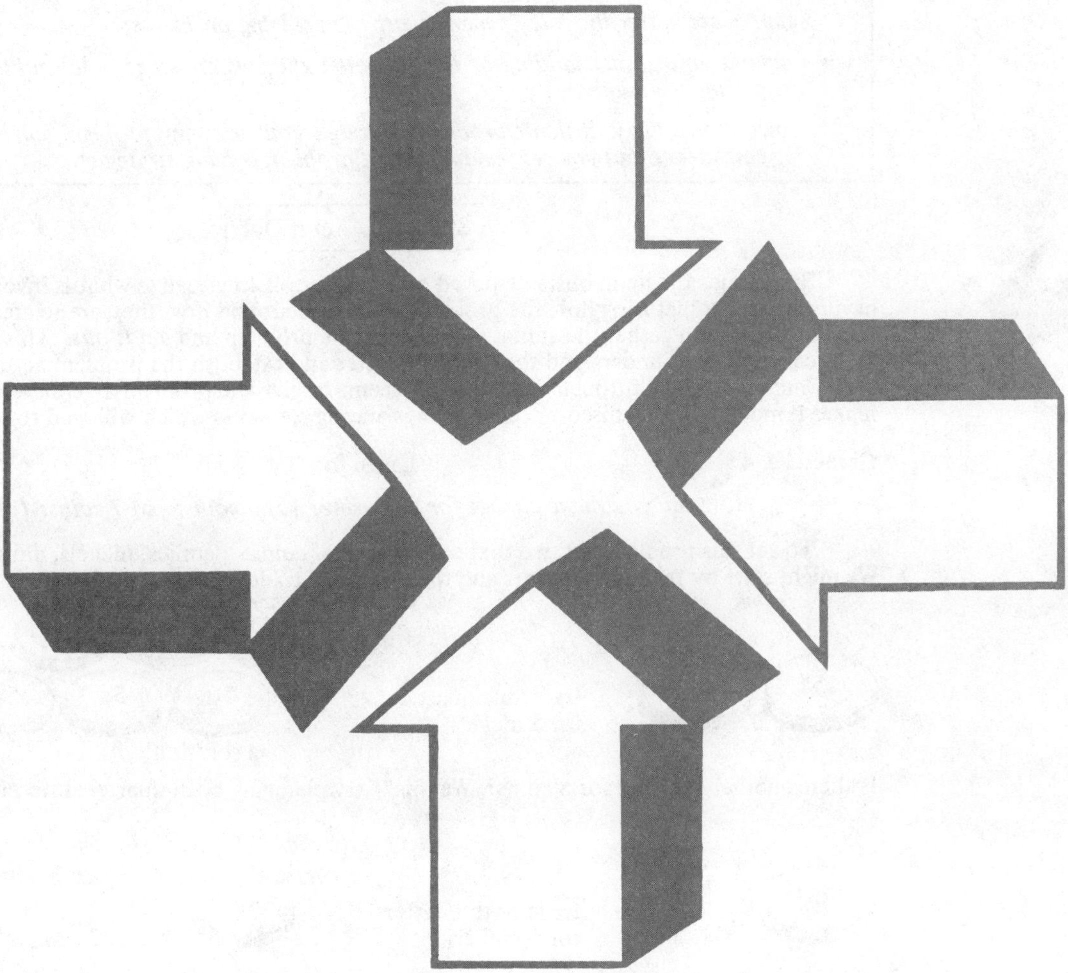

STRATEGIES–PART II

The next set of strategies consists of some of the most powerful tools used to solve complex problems. Yet they are actions familiar to young children. This points to an interesting paradox: the more difficult that a problem appears, the more elementary the method may be that is needed to make it understandable and solvable.

As a result of studying this section, you will be able to:

- *use four additional strategies in solving problems: act it out, make a model, guess and check, and working backwards;*
- *appreciate better the role of manipulatives in solving problems;*
- *expand your understanding of the educated guess as an acceptable problem solving technique;*
- *solve increasingly difficult problems through your growing problem solving confidence and your expanding use of problem solving strategies.*

Strategy: Act it Out

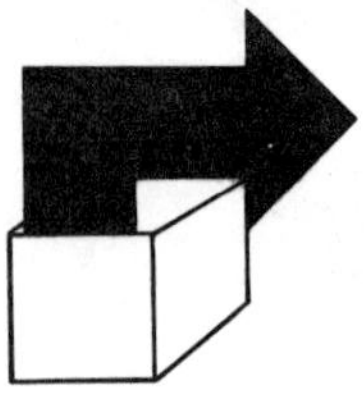

Sometimes the main obstacle posed by a problem is to visualize what is involved. We may be having difficulty picturing how the problem actions occur and how they are related. To overcome this hurdle, we can gather the actual materials of the problem and *act it out*. This physical involvement can help us to understand the problem better and establish the problem actions more firmly in our minds. "Going through the motions" seems to give the problem a "concreteness" that makes it much easier to discover relationships among elements which will lead to solution.

Grades 3 & 4 Change for 50¢

How can you make change for 50¢ using: (a) 6 coins; (b) 7 coins; (c) 8 coins?

To act this problem out, we first collect several coins: pennies, nickels, dimes, and quarters. We might start by taking 2 quarters and then begin to trade coins.

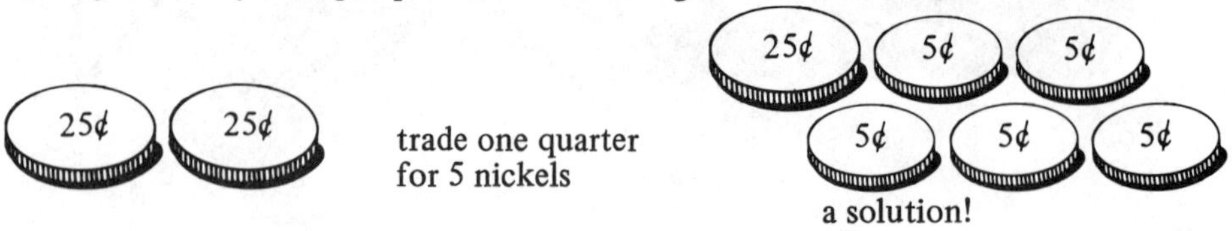

Is there another solution for 6 coins? We might try changing both quarters into nickels.

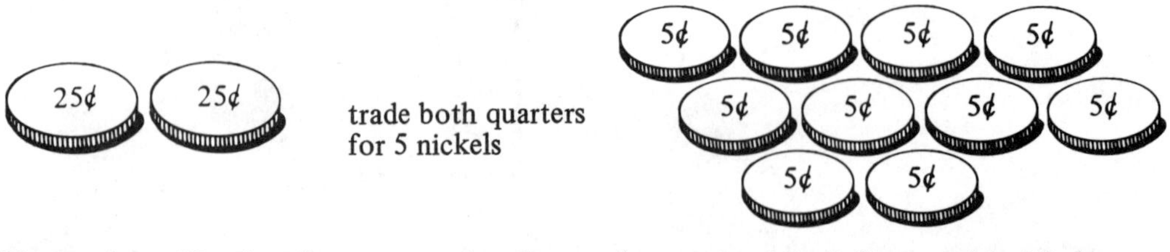

Now we have 10 coins. So we try again. Change the quarters into 2 dimes and 1 nickel.

More trading *(acting it out)* should convince us that these are the only solutions. We leave as a challenge for you making change consisting of 7 coins (one solution) and 8 coins (two solutions).

Any Grades Horse Trading

A man buys a horse for $60, sells it for $70, buys it back for $80, and sells it for $90. How much does the man make or lose in the horse trading business?

Try to solve this problem by *acting it out.* Get two friends, one to act as the horse. Using real or play money, carry through the transactions of the problem. Now stop and solve the problem.

Did your answer surprise you? Studies on this well-researched problem [Maier, 1970, p. 123] indicate that more than 60 percent of the adults who attempt the problem obtain a wrong answer.

You should have decided that the difference in the amount of money you have at the beginning and end of the transactions determines how much you make or lose.

The following pictures show the results of each transaction. They assume that you start with $100 and the other person $60 and the horse (both amounts are arbitrary but large enough to complete all transactions).

You started with $100 and no horse. You finished with $120 and no horse. So you made $120 - $100 = $20.

Strategy: Make a Model

Acting out the conditions of a problem is not always possible or convenient. However, it may still be important to visualize problem elements and actions. In such cases, it is sometimes possible to *make a model* of the problem. Easily accessible objects can represent the harder to obtain or awkward to use real objects of the problem. Simple actions can replace more complicated activities of the problem.

For example, in the preceding problem we suggested using a person to represent a horse since using an actual horse would be inconvenient. Moreover, no ownership papers exchanged hands in our problem discussion as they would in a real transaction. Nonessential elements of the real situation were dismissed while relevant actions and problem components were simplified through modeling.

In using *make a model,* you should strive to select objects or actions to model those from the actual problem situation that: (a) represent the situation accurately, and (b) permit you to relate the simplified problem to the actual problem.

Grades 3 & 4 Wheels and Riders

I counted 7 cycle riders and 19 cycle wheels go past my house Saturday morning. How many bicycles and how many tricycles passed my house?

Since we are interested in wheels, an appropriate selection to represent them might be round objects that are readily available and sufficient in number. We might choose pennies to represent wheels. Then our cycles are modeled by:

To begin the problem, we count out 19 pennies to represent the 19 wheels. Arbitrarily we begin to form bicycles and tricycles until all "wheels" are used.

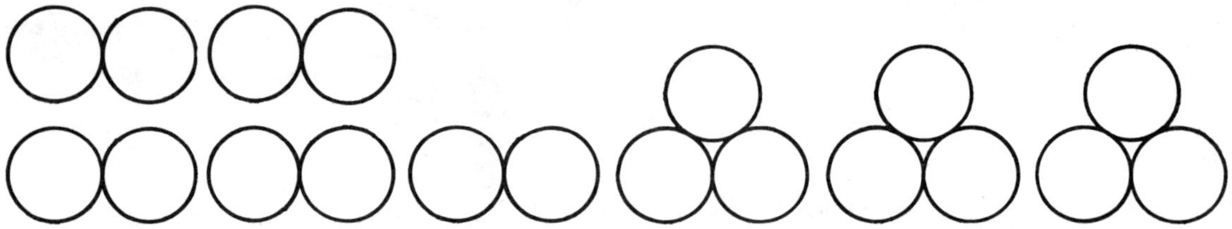

Counting we find that we have 8 cycles instead of 7. Therefore, we have to rearrange wheels to form fewer cycles. Changing tricycles into bicycles will not make fewer cycles, but changing bicycles to tricycles will reduce the number of cycles.

So we take two bicycles to form another tricycle.

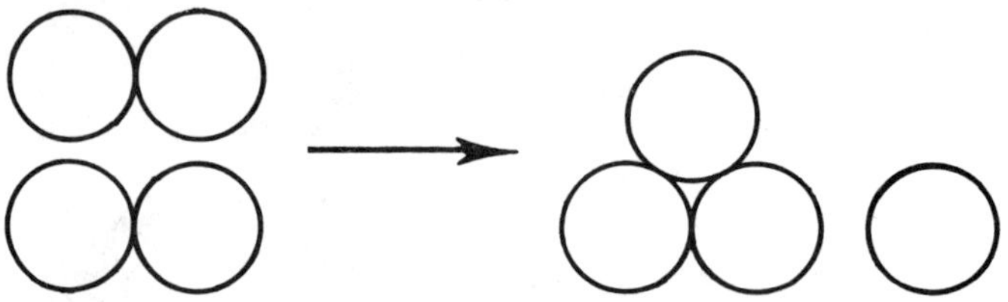

Now we have a wheel left over. Therefore, we add it to another bicycle forming another tricycle. Now we have 5 tricycles and 2 bicycles, the required answer.

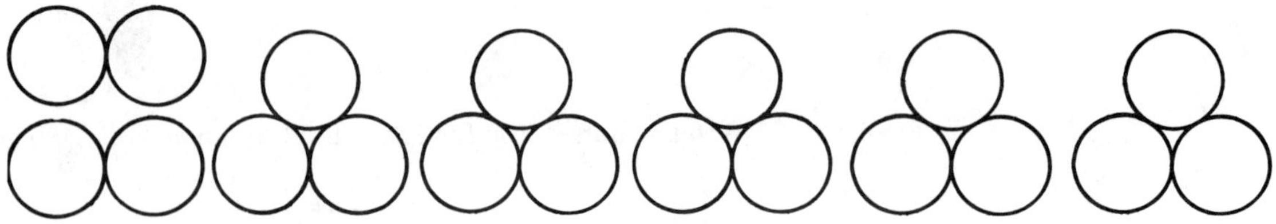

Grades 5 & 6

Consider the gears at the right. If A turns 3 times, how many times will C turn? In what direction?

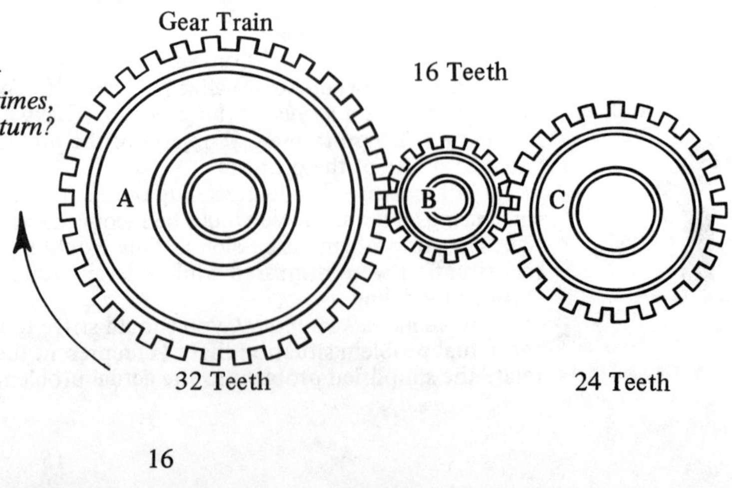

This problem can be answered arithmetically. But to practice *making a model,* trace these gears on another piece of paper, paste to cardboard, and then cut out. Attach the cardboard gears to a flat surface with pins. Carry out the conditions of the problem.

Now stop and do it.

The answer to this problem is found in Appendix B. If you did not cut the gears out, you deprived yourself of the benefit of discovering other related problems that you could explore once you have the gears.

Activity IV: Write a related gear problem and give it to a fellow teacher. After he or she has worked on the problem, produce your gears. Discuss your feelings about solving the problem with and without the model.

Strategy: Guess and Check

One of the least appreciated strategies is *guess and check.* Guessing for the solution of a problem is frequently associated with aimless casting about for an answer. We do not advocate blind guessing, but we wholeheartedly do encourage educated guesses.

What is the difference?

An educated guess is based upon the problem solver's careful attention to pertinent aspects of the problem, though not necessarily in a formal manner. This information is assimilated with his previous related experiences to produce a hypothesized answer which the guesser has some reason to expect to be "in the right ball park."

As a strategy, the key element is *and check.* In other words, the problem solver makes an educated guess **and then checks** it against the problem conditions to determine how to improve his guess. He repeats this process until he has an acceptable answer.

Grades 4 & 5 Postage Due

It costs 10¢ to mail a postcard and 16¢ for a letter. Billie told me he wrote 12 friends and spent $1.62 for postage. How many letters and how many postcards did he write?

We notice first that at 16¢ per letter, 10 letters would take virtually all of the $1.62 so fewer than 10 letters must be used. Our first guess is 8 letters. *Using a table,* we organize our information, (letters + postcards = 12).

Letters		Postcards		Totals	
Number	Cost @ 16¢	Number	Cost @ 10¢	Number	Cost
8	$1.28	4	$0.40	12	$1.68

Since the total cost is too much, we improve our guess by selecting fewer letters and correspondingly more postcards.

Letters		Postcards		Totals	
Number	Cost @ 16¢	Number	Cost @ 10¢	Number	Cost
8	$1.28	4	$0.40	12	$1.68
7	$1.12	5	$0.50	12	$1.62 *

By two guesses and checks, we find that Billie wrote 7 letters and 5 postcards.

Grades 4 & 5 Domino Donuts

Arrange the four dominoes below into a domino donut so all sides equal the same sum (not necessarily the same sum as that of the example).

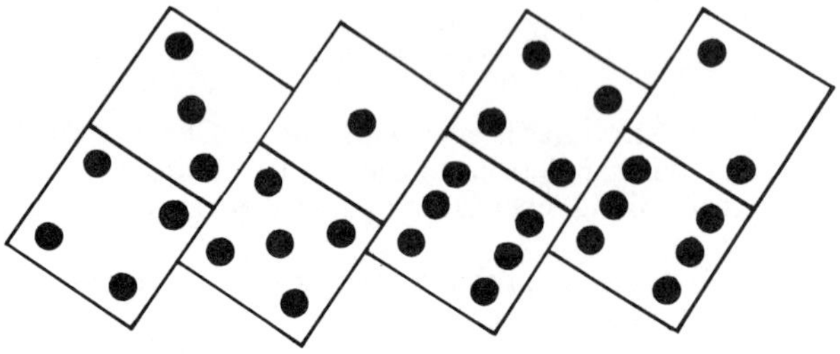

EXAMPLE

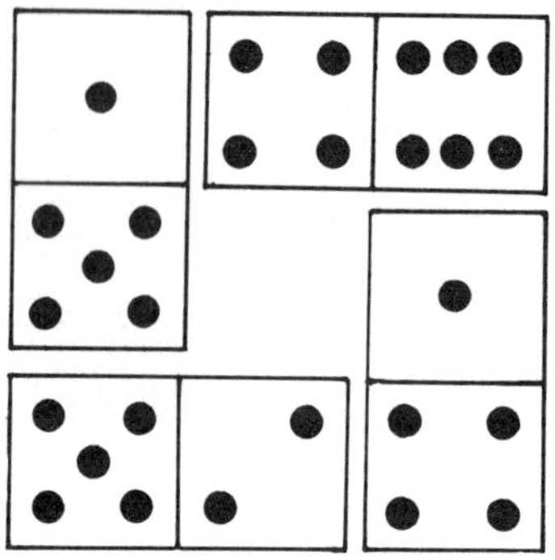

All sums are 11.

Now it is your turn to use *guess and check* to solve a problem. Stop reading and solve this problem.

If you are having difficulty with the problem, try using another strategy with guess and check – *make a model.* Stop reading and solve the problem.

If you still have not solved the problem, try to form sums of 12. The correct answer is given in Appendix B, page 51.

Strategy: Work Backwards

Some problems are posed in such a way that you are given the final conditions of an action and are asked for a condition state that occurred earlier. Or in working toward a solution, you may be able to determine how an action ends and then work backwards to a desired intermediate condition faster than starting from the beginning. When either of these situations exists, *working backwards* is a valuable strategy to employ.

Grades 7 & 8 Barrel Pouring

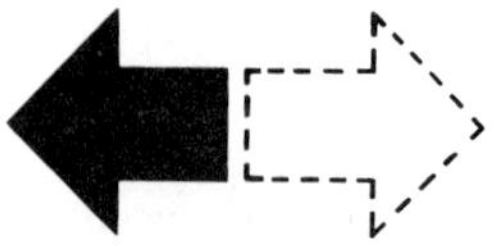

Two barrels A and B contain unspecified amounts of cider, A containing more than B. From A pour into B as much cider as B already contains. Then from B pour into A as much cider as A now contains. Finally, pour from A into B as much cider as B presently has. Both barrels now contain 64 liters of cider. How many liters of cider were in each barrel at the start of the process?

Confused? You should be. Remember that a problem solver must be willing to be perplexed. The advantage to using strategies to solve problems is that they provide you something to try, an entry action to the problem.

The key feature to note in this problem is that a series of actions are described in which we know what occurs at the end. We are asked to determine the initial state. These are the necessary conditions for *working backwards.*

Therefore, we start with the final condition, 64 liters in barrel A and 64 liters in barrel B, and carry out all pourings in the reverse direction!

Problem Statement	Reverse Pouring	Contents at this point
		FINAL CONDITION: A 64 L, B 64 L
Finally, pour from A into B as much cider as B presently has.	Pour from B into A half of the cider now in B.	A 96 L, B 32 L
Then from B pour into A as much cider as A now contains.	Pour from A into B half of the cider now in A.	A 48 L, B 80 L
From A pour into B as much cider as B already contains.	Pour from B into A half of the cider in B.	A 88 L, B 40 L
		INITIAL CONDITION

Therefore, barrel A started with 88 liters of cider and barrel B began with 40 liters. The final test for this solution is whether we can start with these volumes, work through the pourings stated in the problem, and finish with 64 liters in each barrel. We leave this as an exercise for the skeptical reader.

Now it is your turn again with a somewhat easier problem.

Grades 3 & 4

Predict the Number

If you were to continue the number pattern until you get to the star, what number would you put in the star's square?

Can you determine this number without filling in or counting all the numbers between?

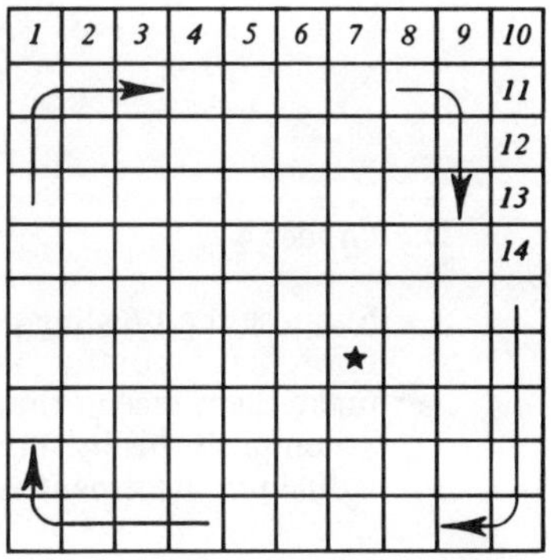

Hint: how many small squares does the large square contain? Where is square 100? Stop reading and solve the problem.

This is an example of a problem where it is easier to determine the final condition state and to work backwards to the intermediate state sought.

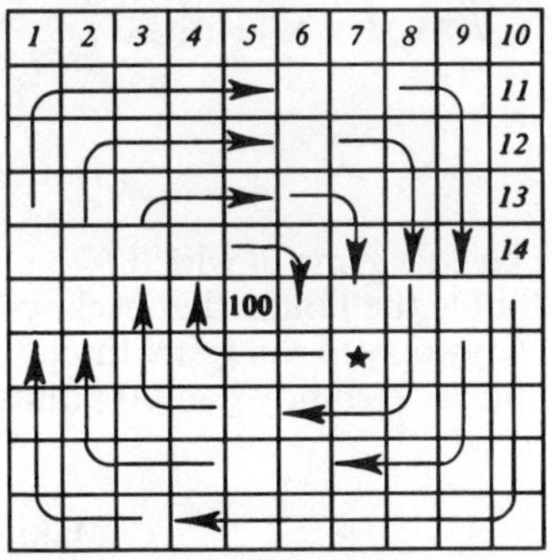

We can locate the square where 100 goes and simply count backward. The star's square will be 91.

Now it is time again to challenge you with a set of problems for which you have to select an appropriate strategy. Generally, *act it out, make a model, guess and check,* or *work backwards* can be used singly or in combination with another strategy to solve these challenge problems.

Challenge Problems Set II

A. Grades 3 & 4 **Removing Sticks**

Place 16 popsicle sticks, as shown, to form 8 small triangles. Now take away 4 sticks so as to leave 4 small triangles. No sticks may be left that are not part of a triangle.

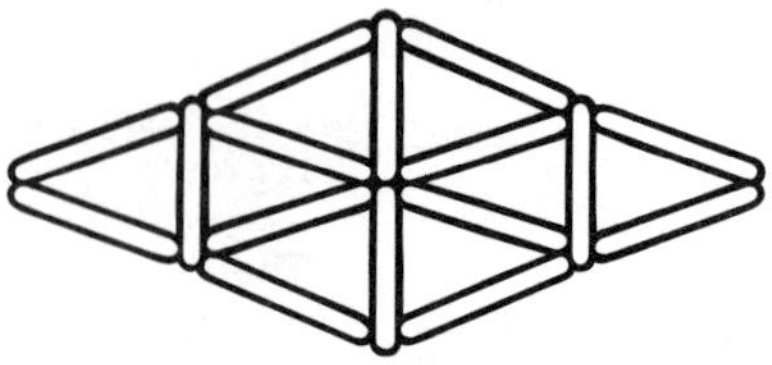

B. Grades 4 & 5 **Fox, Goose, and Corn**

A man, a fox, a goose, and some corn are on one side of a river with only a boat for crossing. The goal is to transfer man, fox, goose, and corn across the river using the boat which will carry the man and only one other thing. Unfortunately, the fox and goose cannot be left alone on either side nor can the goose and corn. How can the river crossing be accomplished?

C. Grades 7 & 8 **Calf's Pen**

A small pasture is to be fenced off with 96 meters of new fencing along an existing fence, using the existing fence as one side of a rectangular enclosure. What are the dimensions of the pasture of largest area that the new fencing will enclose?

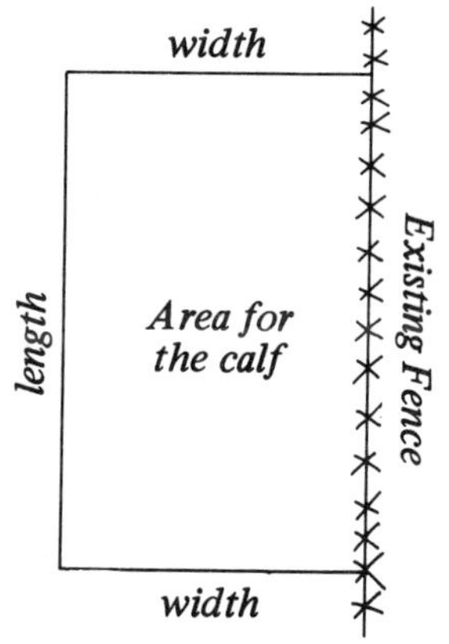

D. Grades 4 & 5 **Bowling Pins**

Suppose the bowling pins shown have been placed improperly, pointing in the wrong direction. To make them face in the opposite direction, can you accomplish this by moving just three pins? Individual pin placement is not important.

Now this way

Should be this way

E. Grades 8 & 9 **Double the Stake**

Three boys played a game in which two of them won and one lost on each play. The boy who lost had to double the points that each winner had at that time by subtracting from his own points. The boys played the game three times, each winning twice and losing once. At the end of three plays, each boy had 40 points. How many points did each player have to start?

F. Grades 6 & 7 **Making Cylinders**

Two rectangular sheets 15 cm x 24 cm and 12 cm x 30 cm are to be rolled to form cylinders (bottoms to be attached later). What is the height and diameter of the cylinder of maximum volume that can be formed using either of these sheets?

A PEDAGOGICAL TIME-OUT: OTHER PROBLEM SOLVING APPROACHES

There are other problem solving techniques used at the elementary and intermediate levels in addition to the strategies that these materials discuss. At this time, we pause in our strategies work to discuss two of these alternate approaches, their strengths, weaknesses, and relationships to strategies.

The Polya 4–Stage Model

Most elementary textbook series employ a 4-stage problem solving approach (sometimes 5- or 6-steps) that is an adaptation of a problem solving model usually attributed in mathematics to George Polya.*

The four stages in this approach and their descriptions are:

1. SEE	What is the problem? What are you trying to find? What is happening? What are you asked to do?
2. PLAN	What do you know? What operation should you use? What do you need to do to solve the problem? How can you obtain more information or data to seek the solution?
3. DO	Carry out the plan you choose. Revise it if necessary. If the plan does not work as anticipated, go back to the PLAN or SEE stages and try again.
4. CHECK	Compare your answer to the problem conditions. Did you find or do that which was requested? Does the solution meet all the conditions? Does it make sense – is it reasonable? Is this the only solution to the problem? If the answer is not exact, is it close enough?

The strengths of this model are twofold. It makes the problem solver aware of the significant stages in the solution process of a problem. Secondly, it provides an organizational framework for very complex or lengthy problems that helps the problem solver organize his efforts.

For very young problem solvers, a SEE, PLAN, DO, CHECK approach can help them begin to see problem solving as a process that consists of several interrelated actions as compared to the single-action format of a computational exercise. The key word for each stage can act as a guide for the young child, suggesting each succeeding action that he needs to accomplish to solve the problem. For a very complex problem such as *"What can be done to correct this city's air pollution problems?"* the stages represent the major blocks of activity that must be undertaken to make a coordinated attack on the problem. Each phase, SEE, PLAN, DO, CHECK, will consist of numerous smaller problems that will in turn require problem solving of another magnitude.

The Polya model has limitations, however. Many problems encountered by the individual are not large or lengthy ones requiring a sophisticated organizational attack. They are relatively short, simple ones which are frequently solved without the individual ever consciously employing any problem solving techniques. Listing specific stages such as SEE, PLAN, DO, CHECK are apt to be more time-consuming than helpful for such problems.

Another difficulty arises through oversimplification of the model. Some persons mistakenly perceive the stages to be steps and attempt to equate SEE, PLAN, DO, CHECK with specific actions. SEEing the problem becomes "reading the problem"; PLANning the problem reduces to "selecting the operation." For some elementary story problems, this simplification of the model is successful. However, as problems grow in complexity, it becomes apparent that such a formula or recipe application of the model is inadequate. The key words for each stage of the model do not indicate the actions that one must perform. They simply suggest an action state that is needed.

*George Polya is the noted author of **How to Solve It** and other problem solving books.

Many actions may be required to understand the problem fully, and these actions may be unique to the problem. The actions may vary from problem solver to solver.

Furthermore, the stages of the model are not discrete. In attempting to generate more information to understand the problem better, one may move without notice into the planning stage. Or once the problem is understood, the task connected with finding the solution may become apparent. The problem becomes a mere exercise. We know what needs to be done and which series of actions will accomplish it.

What, then, do you do to attain the action stages of the model? The answer is to ask yourself the types of questions associated with each key word of the model. Then select a strategy or strategies to help answer those questions. The strategies are action-oriented. They do something to the problem. Strategies alter the problem information, organize it, expand it, make it more easily understood. As such, strategies are the tools for solving problems and the Polya model the blueprint.

With sufficient practice, strategies become good mental habits. When the problem does not warrant use of the 4-stage model, you select and apply a strategy to solve the problem. Frequently, you will be unaware of having selected a specific strategy. For more difficult problems, strategies become the means by which each stage of the Polya model is realized. More formal planning and conscious thought may be required.

Classificatory Problem Solving

A second approach widely used at the elementary level can be called classificatory problem solving. It entails recognition of a problem situation as fitting a particular problem class for which the solver already knows certain procedures. Some familiar classifications that enjoy widespread use are: time-rate-distance problems, proportion problems, percent problems, finding the average problems, interest-rate-time-principal problems. Problems may also be classified according to the learner's stage of development. Addition, subtraction, fraction, mixed number, money, or time problem classifications assume grade level meanings and relevance in terms of the most recently studied concepts or computational techniques.

Classifying is an important process in many kinds of learning experiences. It helps us associate new data with related known information. It helps us catalogue searches so that we do not have to consider each case or item separately. It allows us the luxury of not having to "reinvent the wheel."

We tend to classify all kinds of information resulting from a problem situation whether or not we overtly label the situation as a type. One of the first questions a good problem solver considers is "Have I ever encountered a problem similar to this one?" Or "Are there any aspects of this problem that I already know how to handle?" This kind of check-back activity to previous problem solving experiences is ongoing and highly desirable.

Therefore, classification is both an activity in the problem solving process and a method for broadening one's problem solving capabilities. Certainly, there are numerous predictable kinds of problem situations that reoccur with sufficient frequency to make it worthwhile to study how to deal with variations of these situations. Recognition of a problem as a special case of a known problem class can greatly decrease the time required for solution.

However, problems are not always recognizable by types as we deal with them initially. If classifying of a problem becomes a necessary step for beginning an attack on that problem, many problem solving efforts are likely to be thwarted. Overdependence upon classificatory problem solving can also entice the problem solver into a rote-like attitude toward problems. He may try to force problem situations to conform to those special classifications that he knows rather than adjusting to the unique conditions of the given problem. A classificatory problem solver also may not be as likely to perceive similarities among different problem types.

Strategies are natural complements to classificatory problem solving. Free of any association with specific problems or problem types, strategies can be used to get one started on any problem. After initial application of strategies in the problem comprehension stage, a problem may be recognized as a special type for which classificatory problem solving can then be employed. Strategies also tend to encourage the solver to attempt to classify a problem after its solution as well as before. The looking back effect of certain strategies* encourages the problem solver to look for commonalities among seemingly different problems. The result of this retrospection leads to a deeper understanding of problem solving and a much stronger ability to solve new problems.

Our efforts in this book are not intended to replace either of the two alternate problem solving approaches discussed here or other formal or informal methods that you currently use. Rather, we feel that a strategies approach will improve not only your general problem solving capabilities but also strengthen other approaches that you may already be using.

Activity V: In Activity I, page 5, you wrote five sentences expressing your views about problem solving. Review those sentences now that you have had an opportunity to study and experience problem solving through these materials. How have your current perceptions changed from your previous ideas?

Activity VI: Discuss with a colleague or group of teachers your views about the relative importance of the Polya model, classificatory, and strategies approaches to problem solving. You may wish to focus some of the following factors in your discussion: grade level, order of introduction, relationship to content, allocation of instructional time, student ability levels, desired competencies.

*Looking back strategies will be considered in depth in **A Resource for Problem Solving.**

STRATEGIES–PART III

The five strategies of this section are those traditionally associated in the elementary program with story problems. However, they represent appropriate actions useful for beginning or solving any kind of problem. We have already seen how other strategies are helpful in story situations.

> As a result of studying this section, you will be able to:
>
> - *use five new strategies in solving problems: make a drawing, diagram, or graph; select appropriate notation; restate the problem; identify wanted, given, and needed information; write an open sentence;*
> - *employ strategies in combinations of two or more to solve a problem;*
> - *appreciate the more organized manner in which you go about solving problems.*

Strategy: Make a drawing, diagram, or graph

Many problems present the solver with the difficulty of organizing the given (or obtainable) information in such a way that he can determine its relationship to the solution. Earlier, we considered a similar kind of need when we searched for a pattern and constructed a table. However, the relationship between the given information and the desired solution need not involve a pattern. Moreover, a table may not be the most appropriate way to make these relationships apparent!

Making a drawing, diagram, or graph can often be a more effective means of depicting the information of a problem. Situations involving geometric ideas particularly can be clarified by making a drawing.

Grades 6 & 7 A Height Phenomenon

When standing atop an object, 10–20 feet high, and looking down, it appears much higher than when you are below the object and looking up. Is there a physical explanation for this or is it just psychological?

If we make a drawing of this situation, we show a stick person atop the object and indicate his line of vision. We also show the stick person below the object looking up.

Putting in the lines of sight, we observe that there is a geometric difference due to the height of the person. The difference in heights observed at A and B is equal to twice the person's eye height (distance from his feet to his eyes). Therefore, it is not entirely psychological.

Making a drawing made the explanation for this common observation readily apparent.

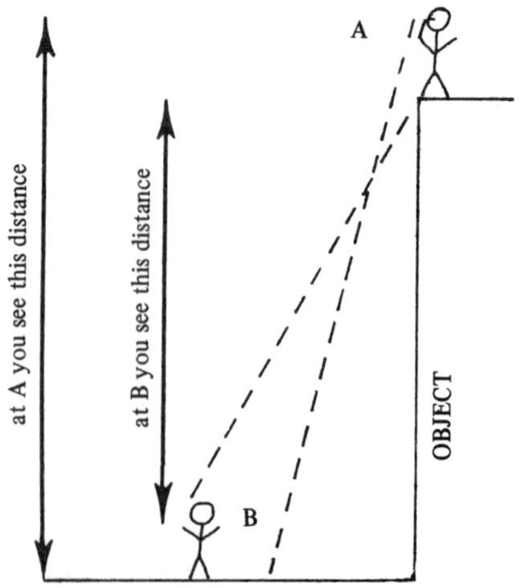

A problem may be easily solved by one person without the aid of a drawing, but its use may greatly assist another. The following problem can be answered without the use of a drawing, but it is easier if you first make a sketch.

Grades 4 & 5 Watching your Watch

Adrienne set her watch at 7:30 am. At 1:30 pm she noticed her watch had lost 4 minutes. Predict how many minutes her watch will lose by 7:30 am the next day.

Stop reading and solve the problem by making a drawing.

The very nature of a clock, since it is not a decimal system, makes the use of a drawing appropriate here. After drawing clock faces representing 7:30 am and 1:30 pm, we can easily determine that 6 hours have elapsed. Using the ratio, 4 minutes lost per 6 hours, we can predict 16 minutes lost for 24 hours. Or we can continue to use the drawings of the clock faces, adding four minute losses for each 6 hour movement on the clock face: (4 + 4 + 4 + 4) minutes = 16 minutes.

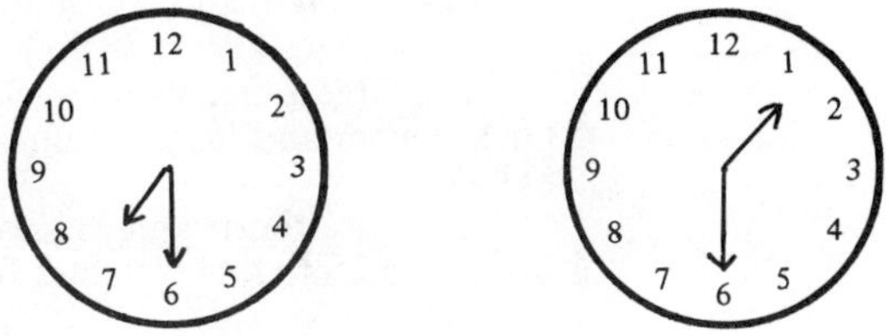

As a third example of this strategy, let us reconsider a somewhat more difficult question from the challenge problems of the preceding section.

Grades 7 & 8 Calf's Pen

A small pasture is to be fenced off with 96 meters of new fencing along an existing fence, using the existing fence as one side of a rectangular enclosure. What are the dimensions of the largest area that the new fencing will enclose?

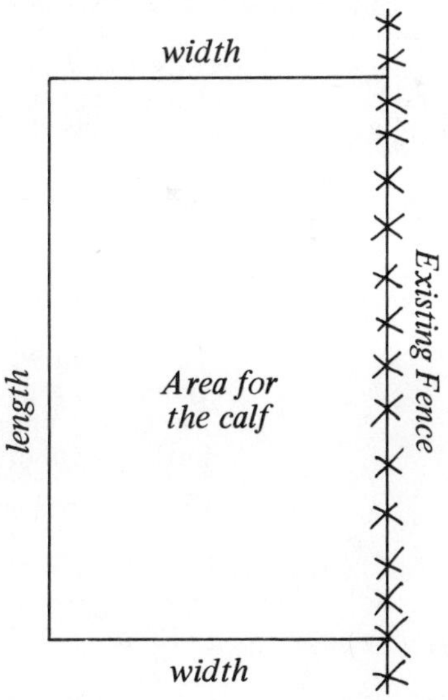

If this problem were not given with a diagram, our first order of business would appropriately be to draw one. Since this is a relatively difficult problem, we should not be surprised to see several strategies involved in its solution. The first use of a strategy, *making a drawing,* is important in being able to conceptualize the problem.

As we study the drawing and reread the problem, the task becomes: divide the 96 meters of new fence into one length and two widths so that the area of the rectangle is as large as possible. *Guessing and checking* seems to be an appropriate way to generate additional information. *Using a table* will help us to organize our efforts.

If we guess a length, say 20 meters, half of the fencing left (96 - 20 = 76) will have to be used for each width. We can then determine the area for an enclosure of those dimensions:

$$\begin{aligned} A &= 1 \times w \\ &= 20 \times 38 \\ &= 760 \text{ m}^2 \end{aligned}$$

Trying other length values, we can begin to fill in the table.

Length	Width $\frac{1}{2}$ (96 - length)	Area length x width
20 m	38 m	760 m^2
26 m	35 m	910 m^2
32 m	32 m	1024 m^2
38 m	29 m	1102 m^2
44 m	26 m	1144 m^2
50 m	23 m	1150 m^2
56 m	20 m	1120 m^2
62 m	17 m	1054 m^2

note: length and width are relative terms

The largest area listed in the table is 1150 m^2 (associated with a length of 50 m and width of 23 m). Larger and smaller values for the length produced smaller areas. But is 1150 m^2 the largest area?

If we use the strategy *make a graph,* we can better visualize how the area changed with arbitrarily selected table values for the length.

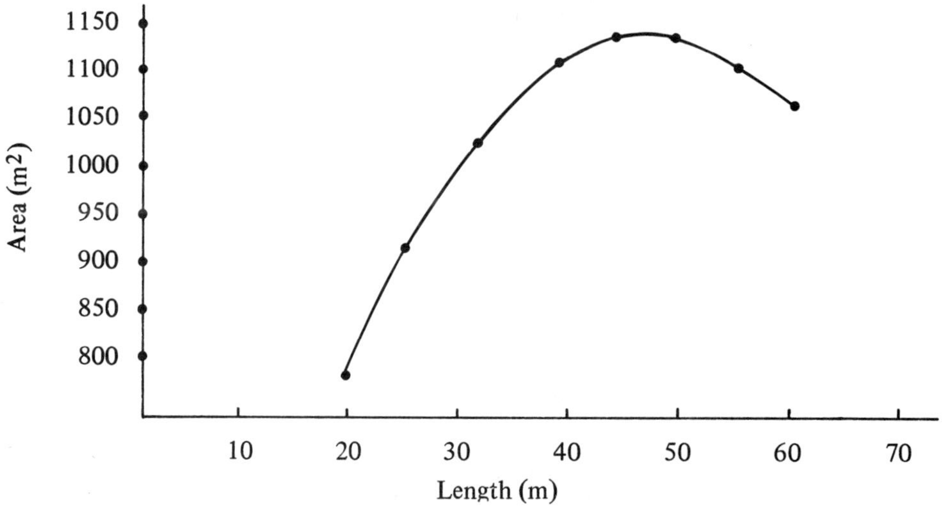

When we draw a smooth line through the points on the graph, we notice behavior and symmetry that causes us to believe a maximum area will be achieved for a length of about 50 m. Depending upon our needs, we can return to the table and refine our answers by *guess and check* in the neighborhood of lengths of 50 m.

Length	Width $\frac{1}{2}$ (96 - length)	Area length x width
46 m	25 m	1150 m^2
48 m	24 m	1152 m^2
50 m	23 m	1150 m^2
checking		
47 m	24.5 m	1151.5 m^2
49 m	23.5 m	1151.5 m^2

With some confidence we can now say that the maximum area is 1152 m^2 for a length of 48 m and a width of 24 m.

In reflection on this more difficult problem, we note that we had to use strategies in several ways. *Guess and check* provided us with additional information in trying to find a solution. *Using a table* was helpful in organizing this information. We *systematically account for (all) possibilities* by regularly increasing the length guessed to observe the effect on the area. *Making a graph* served to convince us that a maximum area was going to be achieved by a length close to 50 m. Returning to *guess and check,* we were able to zero in on the answer.

Strategy: Select Appropriate Notation

Mathematics is a body of knowledge that has as one of its distinguishing characteristics the awesome power to represent very complex ideas and statements with relatively simple symbol combinations. A mathematical sentence such as $4 + 5 = 5 + 4$ conveys five separate ideas in very compact form: the notions of four and five, the operation of addition, the condition of equality, and the total statement that order does not matter when adding four and five.

In using mathematics to solve problems, we draw upon our knowledge of symbols and ideas they represent to put a problem into a form that can be more easily handled. When a problem has been put into symbolic form, we can operate on the symbols according to prescribed rules of mathematics without consciously considering the ideas the symbols represent. After a prescribed condition state has been achieved, we interpret the existing symbol statement in terms of the ideas of the original problem.

The selection of symbols that will represent ideas in a problem can directly influence the difficulty of the resulting symbol problem. This refers not only to selection of good symbols to use but also to the representation of the problem itself in terms of a mathematical model.

Consider the following problem.

Grades 5 & 6 Chess Club

At the first meeting of the Chess Club, the 10 members decided that everyone in the club should play everyone else one time to determine the five best players for interschool competitions. How many games had to be played?

Since every member plays all other members, it might appear that 9 games played by each member times the 10 members yields a total of 90 games. However, first appearances can be deceiving. Suppose we look at the problem in another way.

If we represent people in the club by dots, we need 10 dots.

A game played between two players can be shown by a line segment joining two dots. The real problem can then be posed as a mathematical problem: how many line segments are required to join ten dots.

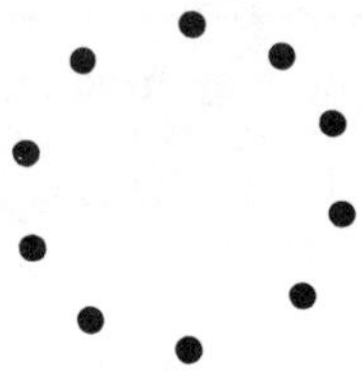

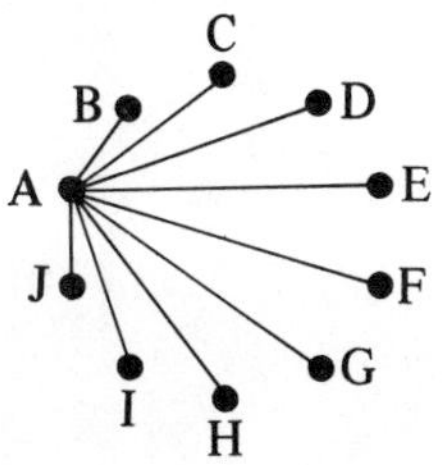

Labeling the points, we can draw all possible segments from A. There are nine such segments

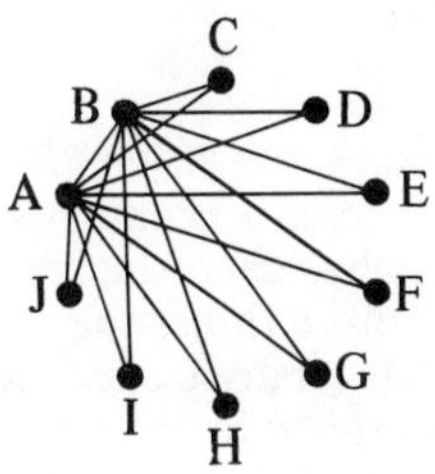

Next, drawing segments from B (we note that B has already been joined to A and counted) eight more line segments are required to connect the other points to B.

Continuing with point C, seven more segments are needed, and so on. Stop and complete a similar diagram.

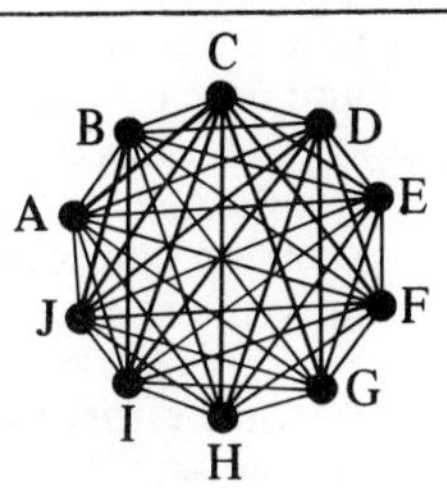

The completed figure looks like that shown at right. If you kept careful count of the segments required from each point, you found $9 + 8 + 7 + 6 + 5 + 4 + 3 + 2 + 1 = 45$

Notice that we *systematically accounted for all possibilities.* Had we drawn the line segments haphazardly, they not only would have been difficult to count but we could easily have missed putting one in.

Now we must reinterpret our notation results in terms of the original problem. The 45 line segments joining 10 dots mean that 45 games are necessary for the 10 Chess Club members to play each other once.

While determining the answer to the problem posed, we stopped focusing on the problem particulars and recast the problem as a geometric one by a wise choice of notation. A bonus in making this change is that the mathematical model chosen to represent the problem helps us see the similarity of this problem to others. For example, finding the number of diagonals for a decagon (10 sides) reduces to essentially the same mathematical problem. (35 = 45 segments - 10 sides). Moreover, the abstraction of the real problem to a mathematical one removes some of the nonessential elements of the situation that might prove distracting.

Our original conjecture proved too large because when Carrie plays Joe, that game is the same game as when Joe plays Carrie. Therefore, only half as many games need be played $\frac{1}{2}$ (90) = 45.

Give careful thought to choosing appropriate notation before solving the next problem.

Grades 4 & 5 At the Brook

Given only two irregularly shaped jars that will hold 7 quarts and 3 quarts of water, describe a sequence of fillings and emptyings that will permit you to come back from the brook with exactly 5 quarts of water.

Now stop reading and work on the problem.

If you need a hint, consider using ordered pairs to represent the water in each jar at a given stage of the pourings. Let the first number represent the water in the 7-quart jar and the second number the water in the 3-quart jar. (0, 3) means 7-quart jar empty and 3 quarts of water in the 3-quart jar.

You may have chosen another notation and problem representation than that involving ordered pairs. However, the actions in your pouring sequence should be the same as those given in one of the following two possibilities.

(0,3) → (3,0) → (3,3) → (6,3) → (7,2) → (0,2) → (2,0) → (2,3) → (5,0)

or

(7,0) → (4,3) → (4,0) → (1,3) → (1,0) → (0,1) → (7,1) → (5,3) → (5,0)

Strategy: Restate the Problem

Given a problem, one of your first tasks is to make it your own. This means that you must internalize what the problem entails before it assumes any meaning for you. You need to determine those things the problem involves, the actions that occur (or are to occur), and that which must generally be accomplished. A good test of your comprehension is whether you can *restate the problem* in your own words without reference to the original problem statement.

Many unsuccessful problem solving attempts stem from too little time spent in defining and understanding the problem. A major source of this failure is a lack of awareness that problem comprehension usually occurs in stages rather than all at once. For example, if a written problem is posed, your first reading of the problem may result only in a general familiarity with the problem so that you can begin to visualize the objects and activities the problem involves. At this stage, you may even wish to de-emphasize specifics.

Following a second reading, you begin mentally to put the problem into your own working terminology as you take into consideration the specifics of the problem. At a third stage of your problem comprehension (not necessarily following a third reading), you reduce the problem to only the relevant ideas involved as you begin to shape the problem into a workable form.

We list *restate the problem* as a strategy, not only because it can help the problem solver start his efforts productively, but also because a restatement will sometimes lead directly to a solution.

Grades 3 & 4 Don't Spend It All at Once

If I start with $10 and spend all but $3, how much do I have left?

Restate this problem in your own words. What is the problem?

While some may consider this a trick question, it can be very useful in convincing you to be sure of what the problem asks.

Consider the following problem. Read it normally three times. At the end of each reading, restate the problem in your words for that reading, and ask yourself if you know enough to solve the problem.

Grades 5 & 6 At the Five and Ten

I bought some items at the Five and Ten store. All the items were the same price and I bought as many items as the number of total cents in the cost of each item. My bill was $2.25. How many items did I buy?

Now stop reading and solve the problem.

On first reading, a representative statement might be: "I bought some items at a store and the total bill was $2.25." (We try to ignore specifics, but some seem to stick in our memory.)

On second reading: "I bought some items at a store. They all cost the same. The total bill is $2.25. How many items were purchased?"

On third reading: "I bought some items that all cost the same amount. I bought as many items as the cost in cents of one item – that is 10¢ cost means 10 items. The total bill was $2.25. How many items were purchased?

When we are able to state the problem in the last format (it may take more than 3 readings), we are ready to formulate the problem for solution. "Some number times itself equals 225 (¢). What is the number?

Guess and check quickly produces 15 as the answer. I bought 15 items at 15¢ for a total cost of $2.25.

Strategy: Identify Wanted, Given, and Needed Information

Informally in the last example, you were mentally classifying certain kinds of information as *given, wanted,* and *needed.* For some problems it is appropriate to more formally identify information. This can help you focus on what is yet to be determined from the problem statement (or your own efforts) as well as listing information so that you may better be able to discover a relationship between what is known and what is required.

Grades 4 & 5 A Cider Bottle

A bottle of cider costs 25 cents. The cider costs 15 cents more than the bottle. How much refund is the bottle worth?

Listing information from the problem we can identify:

GIVEN: cider plus bottle costs 25 cents
cider costs 15 cents more than the bottle

WANTED: cost of bottle

Examining the given and wanted, we need to know how much the cider costs.

NEEDED: how much of the 25¢ is the cider worth?

Rereading the problem, we discover that it does not indicate the cider's cost. Therefore, we will have to use the information in the given to find the bottle's cost without knowing the cider's value.

Guess and check is suggested. If we guess a value for the bottle, the cider costs 15¢ more than this amount. The two amounts must equal 25¢.

Bottle	Cider	Total	Solution
3¢	18¢	21¢	No
4¢	19¢	23¢	No
* 5¢	20¢	25¢	Yes

In actual practice, the above steps would be performed mentally on such a simple problem. But for a more difficult example (or for a younger problem solver), these results may need to be written down.

Strategy: Write an Open Sentence

Writing an open sentence (equation) is one of the most powerful tools available to problem solvers. Quite often, its use is preceded by that of several other strategies. Upon reading (or studying) a problem, we may first begin by *making a drawing* to better visualize the problem. As a result of our drawing, we may *restate the problem* in our own terminology to make it more understandable. Our drawing and further study of the problem may entail listing information as *given, wanted, and needed.* To represent wanted or needed information, we may find it necessary to *select appropriate notation* to represent these quantities. Then, we may be able to perceive a relationship between the given and sought information that we can represent with *an open sentence.*

When the open sentence has been written, we have abstracted the problem from a real to a mathematical situation. A substantial portion of the problem solving process has been completed. By computational means, we should now be able to find a result which can be translated into a problem solution. This is not to lessen the importance of the procedural aspects to occur after the open sentence is written. Great ingenuity can often be employed in solving an open sentence. Under any circumstance, considerable skill is involved. However, problem solving of another dimension occurs after the open sentence is generated. Too frequently, the open sentence is where some perceive problem solving to begin.

Grades 5 & 6 Ant Walk

An ant travels 33 cm in walking completely around the edge of a rectangle. If the rectangle is twice as long as it is wide, how long is each side?

Restating the problem, an ant walks around the edges of a rectangle and we want to know the length and width of the rectangle. At this point, it seems appropriate to *draw* a rectangle.

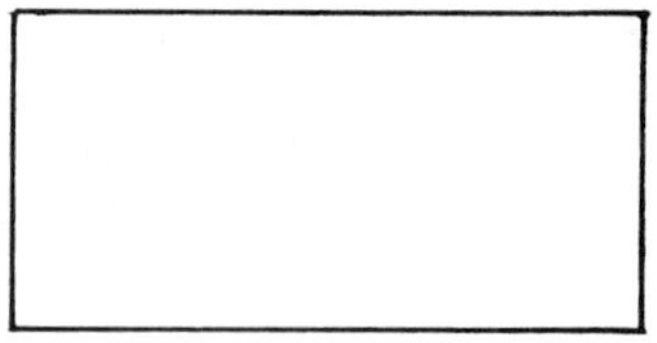

Rereading the problem, we are now ready to *identify given, wanted, and needed information.*

GIVEN: length of walk: 33 cm
rectangle length = twice its width

WANTED: length, width of rectangle

NEEDED: a relationship involving the rectangle's length, width, and distance around (perimeter)

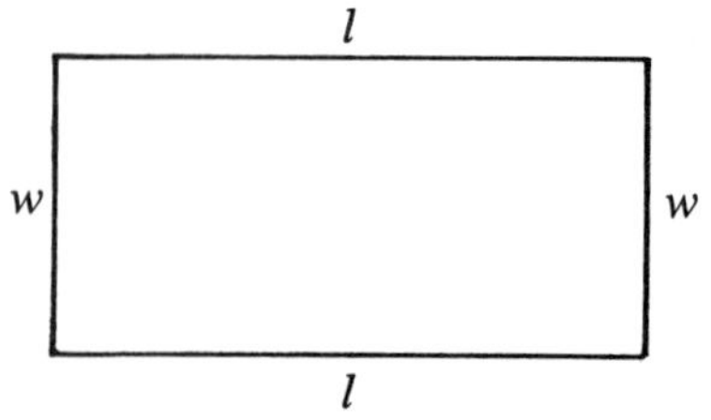

Going back to our rectangle we can *select appropriate notation* in order to write the necessary relationship.

Choosing l for length and w for width, we can write the open sentence $w + l + w + l = 33$. But we know from past experience that two letters (variables) in an open sentence make it more difficult to solve than one letter. Also, we reexamine our given information and realize that the information "length = twice the width" has not been used.

So, we try to find more appropriate notation that uses all of the given. If the length is denoted by l and the length is twice the width, then width is one-half of length, so we could represent width by $\frac{1}{2}l$.

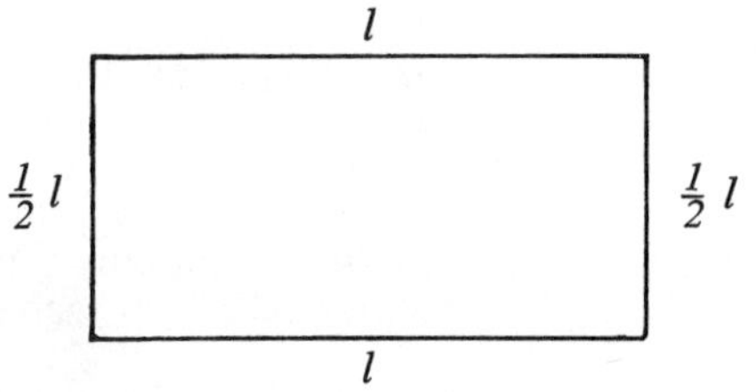

Now our open sentence becomes $\frac{1}{2}l + l + \frac{1}{2}l + l = 33$. From this sentence we can readily find $l = 11$ cm and $\frac{1}{2}l$ (width) = 5.5 cm.

Someone else seeking more appropriate notation may well have selected w for width and consequently used 2w for length. Their open sentence becomes w + 2w + w + 2w = 33 from which w = 5.5 cm and 2w (length) = 11 cm.

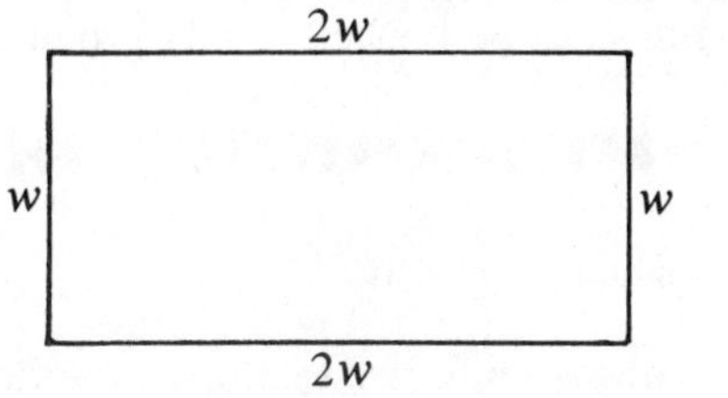

We confess, of course, that we would not go through each step on such a simple problem. However, for illustrative purposes, it serves very nicely to show how individual strategies can reduce the problem at each stage to much simpler decisions.

Try your hand at this problem.

Grades 7 & 8 Better Milk Producers

3 Guernsey cows and 2 Holstein cows give as much milk in 4 days as 2 Guernsey and 4 Holstein cows give in 3 days. Which kind of cow is the better milk producer, Guernsey or Holstein?

Stop reading and try to solve the problem.

If you need a hint, write open sentences for the amount of milk produced by 3 Guernsey and 2 Holstein cows in 4 days and also for the amount produced by 2 Guernsey and 4 Holstein cows in 3 days. How do these amounts compare?

Choosing appropriate notation, let G be the amount of milk produced by a Guernsey cow **each day** and H the amount produced by a Holstein **each day**.
Classifying information from the problem:

GIVEN: 3 Guernsey and 2 Holstein cows and 4 days milk production

2 Guernsey and 3 Holstein cows and 3 days milk production

Amounts of milk produced by two groups of cows in 4 days vs 3 days are equal

WANTED: Is a Guernsey or Holstein the better milk producer on a daily basis?

NEEDED: Expressions and open sentences giving milk production per animal and per group for time periods.

To satisfy our "needed," we observe that if G is the milk production for a Guernsey for one day, then 4G is the milk production for four days for **each** Guernsey cow. There are three such cows in the first group, so they contribute 3 x 4G = 12G amount of milk in four days.

Similarly, a Holstein gives H milk per day or 4H milk per cow for the four days. Therefore, two animals give 2 x 4H or 8H amount of milk in two days.

Adding, 12G + 8H is the milk production of the first group. In a similar manner, we can represent milk production of the second group by 6G + 12H.

Since the given information indicates that the total amounts of milk are equal, we can write the open sentence:

$$12G + 8H = 6G + 12H$$

To simplify this sentence and to answer our question, we recall that an equation is comparable to an equal arm balance. You can remove the same amount from each side without destroying the balance (equality).

Since G's and H's appear on each side of the equal sign, we will remove enough G's and H's from each side so that only G's are left on one side and only H's on the other.

Remove 6G's from each side. The equation becomes

$$6G + 8H = 12H$$

Remove 8H's from each side. The equation becomes

$$6G = 4H$$

Now we examine this last statement to determine which is larger, G or H. Since it takes more G's to equal the milk of fewer H's, Holsteins must be the better milk producers.

Challenge Problems Set III

The following set of challenge problems is divided into two sections. The first five problems can be solved by using one or more strategies from this section. The second five problems may require any of the strategies studied thus far. Refer to the strategy check list on page 33.

A. Grades 5 & 6 — **Fair Shares**

Three girls had already equally divided the cake shown among them when they were joined by a fourth girl who was also hungry. They told her that she could have a share if she could divide the cake into four equal portions by making only one more cut. How did she do it?

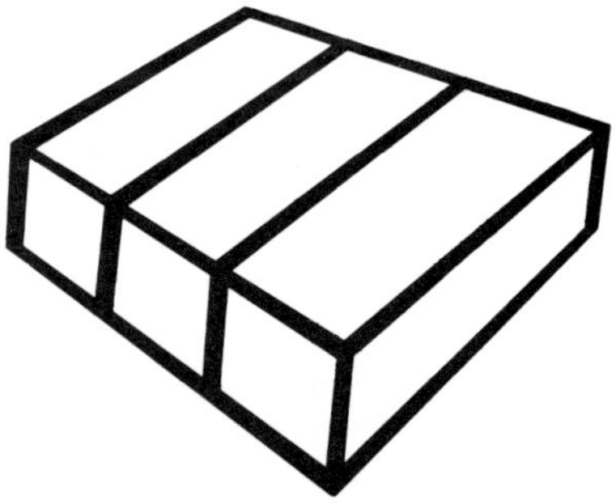

B. Grades 4 & 5 — **Three Beakers**

Start with an 8 liter beaker full of water and two empty beakers of 5 liter and 3 liter capacity. How can you pour from one beaker to another to obtain 4 liters of water in one beaker?

C. Grades 4 & 5 — **Walk or Ride to School**

Each day, Abe either walks to school and rides his bicycle home or rides his bicycle to school and walks home (it always rains sometime each day, and he is not permitted to ride in the rain.) Either way, the round trip takes one hour. If Abe were to ride both ways, it would take 30 minutes. How long would a round trip take if Abe walked both ways?

D. Grades 6 & 7 — **Cans and Marbles**

A can with 40 marbles in it weighed 135 grams. The same can with 20 marbles weighed 75 grams. What is the weight of the can?

E. Grades 5 & 6 — **Heart Beats**

Your heart beats about 80 times each minute. How many times does it beat in one day?

F. Grades 3 & 4 — **How Much Time?**

If it takes two minutes to make a cut, how long would it take to cut a log 20 feet long into ten equal lengths?

G. Grades 3 & 4 — Equal Sums

Move one block to another stack so the sums of all stacks are equal.

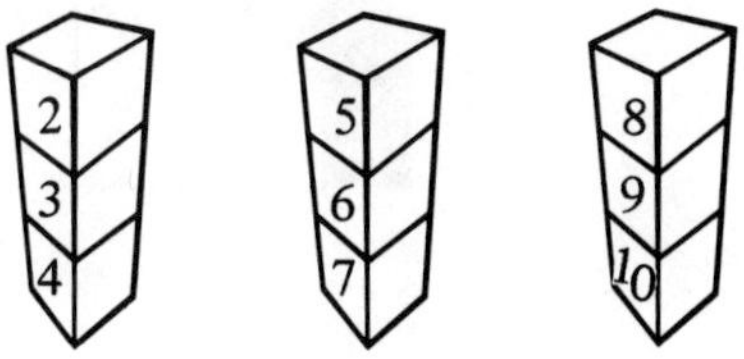

H. Grades 5 & 6 — Who Am I?

I am a counting number. All three of my digits are even and different. The sum of my digits is 12. The product of my digits is less than 40. The sum of my hundred's plus my one's digit is less than my ten's digit. Who am I?

I. Grades 4 & 5 — Football Scoring

During a football game, your team scored 18 points. In how many different ways could your team have made this score?

touchdown (TD) – 6 pts
point after touchdown (PAT) – 1 pt
field goal (FG) – 3 pts
safety (S) – 2 pts

J. Grades 4 & 5 — Tacking up Pictures

What is the least number of thumbtacks that must be used to tack up to 16 pictures so they can all be seen? (Assume each corner of the picture must be tacked.)

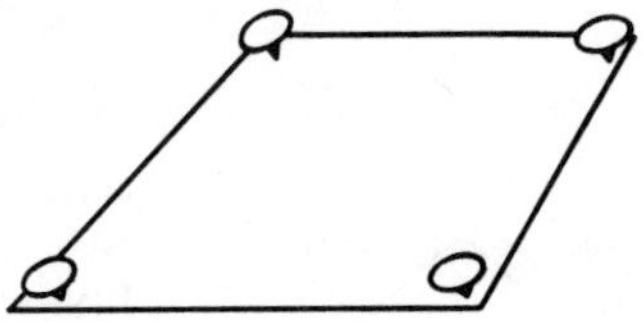

STRATEGY CHECK LIST	
Look for a pattern	___
Construct a table	___
Account for all possibilities	___
Act it out	___
Make a model	___
Guess and check	___
Work backwards	___
Make a drawing	___
Select appropriate notation	___
Restate the problem	___
Identify given, wanted, needed information	___
Write an open sentence	___

STRATEGIES–PART IV

One of the peculiarities of strategies is that they may be used with equal success on very simple problems or very complex ones. This last grouping of strategies contains problem solving techniques that are used by some of the most skillful problem solvers. Yet they are easily learned and usefully employed at the elementary level.

As a result of studying this section, you will be able to:

- *use four new strategies in solving problems: identify a subgoal; solve a simpler problem; change your point of view; check for hidden assumptions;*
- *choose, from a list of 16 strategies, individual or combinations of effective techniques to solve problems;*
- *broaden your perception of problem situations requiring mathematical analyses;*
- *increase your appreciation for the potential for strategy applications to other disciplines.*

Strategy: Identify a Subgoal

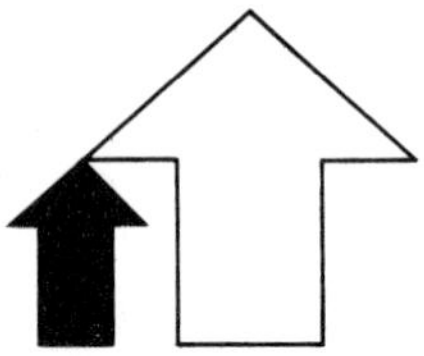

When confronted with a problem, we sometimes can see that its resolution will require a series of actions, each dependent upon the preceding one. We may also face a problem whose specific solution is just beyond reach, but we have strong feelings that certain steps will either produce the solution or give us the additional material to find the answer. In each instance, *identifying a subgoal* is a way of making the problem smaller and getting started.

An ancient Chinese proverb states: "A journey of a thousand miles is begun with the first step." So one should approach some problems. Even though we may not yet have a carefully planned scheme as to how to reach our objective, intuitively we feel that some specific act will get us closer to our goal. Identify this subgoal and pursue it. Upon completion, survey again the original problem. Its solution may now become apparent, or a new subgoal closer to the objective may appear.

Grades 5 & 6 Egyptian Fractions

Egyptians had special rules for their fractions.

- *They used only unit fractions: 1 in the numerator (except for $\frac{2}{3}$, a special case).*
- *They expressed numbers like $\frac{3}{4}$ by using only unit fractions: $\frac{1}{2} + \frac{1}{4}$.*
- *They never used the same unit fraction in an expression more than once.*

Think like an Egyptian to provide a name for the following "modern fractions." Use the number of unit fractions indicated.

a. $\frac{5}{8}$ using 2 unit fractions.

b. $\frac{13}{16}$ using 3 unit fractions

c. $\frac{3}{7}$ using 3 unit fractions.

(a) Looking at $\frac{5}{8}$, our subgoal might be to try to use $\frac{1}{8}$ with whatever remains of $\frac{5}{8}$: $\frac{5}{8} = \frac{1}{8} + \frac{4}{8}$. Immediately, we see that $\frac{4}{8}$ reduces to $\frac{1}{2}$, practically an exercise.

(b) Trying something similar, we remove $\frac{1}{16}$ from $\frac{13}{16}$ and observe that $\frac{13}{16} = \frac{1}{16} + \frac{12}{16}$. Our subgoal becomes: write $\frac{12}{16}$ as two unit fractions. but $\frac{12}{16}$ reduces to $\frac{3}{4}$. Recall this expression from the example, $\frac{3}{4} = \frac{1}{2} + \frac{1}{4}$. Therefore, $\frac{13}{16} = \frac{1}{16} + \frac{1}{4} + \frac{1}{2}$.

(c) Tackling $\frac{3}{7}$, we write $\frac{3}{7} = \frac{1}{7} + \frac{2}{7}$.

Following our previous successful efforts, our task is to rewrite $\frac{2}{7}$ as the sum of two unit fractions. But breaking $\frac{2}{7}$ apart gives: $\frac{2}{7} = \frac{1}{7} + \frac{1}{7}$. We may not use the same unit fraction more than once.

Looking back at $\frac{13}{16}$, we observe that at this step, we **reduced** $\frac{12}{16}$. Since $\frac{2}{7}$ cannot be reduced, why not try the opposite! Rename $\frac{2}{7}$ as a fraction with a larger denominator. Therefore, a reasonable subgoal is to write $\frac{2}{7}$ in higher terms, separating the resulting fraction into two fractions which are (or can be) written as unit fractions.

Rewriting $\frac{2}{7}$ as $\frac{4}{14}$, we try $\frac{2}{7} = \frac{4}{14} = \frac{1}{14} + \frac{3}{14}$ but $\frac{3}{14}$ cannot be rewritten as a single unit fraction.

Trying $\frac{2}{7}$ as $\frac{6}{21}$, we have $\frac{2}{7} = \frac{6}{21} = \frac{1}{21} + \frac{5}{21}$ and again we are stopped.

Writing $\frac{2}{7}$ as $\frac{8}{28}$, we have $\frac{2}{7} = \frac{8}{28} = \frac{1}{28} + \frac{7}{28} = \frac{1}{28} + \frac{1}{4}$ which achieves our subgoal.

Therefore, $\frac{3}{7} = \frac{1}{7} + \frac{1}{28} + \frac{1}{4}$.

Although a procedure for solving the unit fraction problems was not completely apparent at the start of our task, it seemed plausible to attempt to break each fraction down in the way we did. Establishing a subgoal gave us an immediate objective – something we could accomplish that took us closer to the solution.

Grades 3 & 4 Missing Numbers

Fill in the missing numbers in this addition table:

addends (top), addends (left side), sums (inside)

+				
	36			29
32			51	
		61		23
	55		62	

Stop reading and solve the problem.

To solve the problem, you had to be aware that an addition table of this type combines an addend from the numbers along the top with an addend from the numbers along the left side of the table and indicates the sum at the intersection of the appropriate row and column. Therefore, to fill in a missing number, it is necessary to know two parts of an addition statement. Your subgoal becomes: find two numbers in the table that are part of the same addition statement, and fill in the third number.

Acting on this subgoal, the first two steps are:

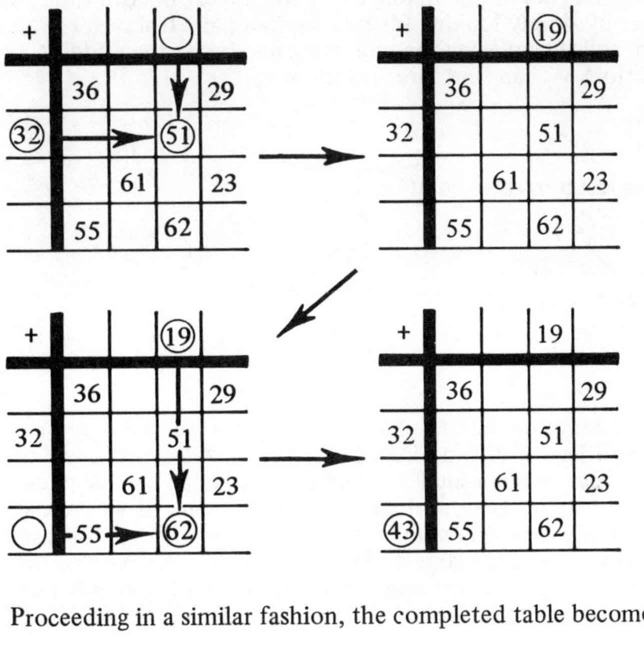

+	12	43	19	5
24	36	67	43	29
32	44	75	51	37
18	30	61	37	23
43	55	86	62	48

Proceeding in a similar fashion, the completed table becomes:

Strategy: Solve a Simpler (or Similar) Problem

Many kinds of problems are interrelated. Knowing how to solve one problem usually means that we can solve another problem that is somewhat similar. In classificatory problem solving, we characteristically study problems by considering simple cases first and advancing to more complex variations of the same type of problem.

In nonclassificatory problem solving, we sometimes forget this bridge between simple and difficult problems. The insight and understanding which permit us to solve more complicated problems are built through the solutions of easier problems. In simpler situations, relationships are easier to see and possibilities few enough to consider one-by-one.

When confronted by a problem with numerous possibilities or complex interrelationships, a useful strategy is to *consider a simpler or similar problem* of the same type. Momentarily, we set aside the original problem to work on the simpler (or similar) case. If that problem can be solved, the same relationships that point toward its solution will often hold for the original problem.

Grades 5 & 6

Spoke Numbers

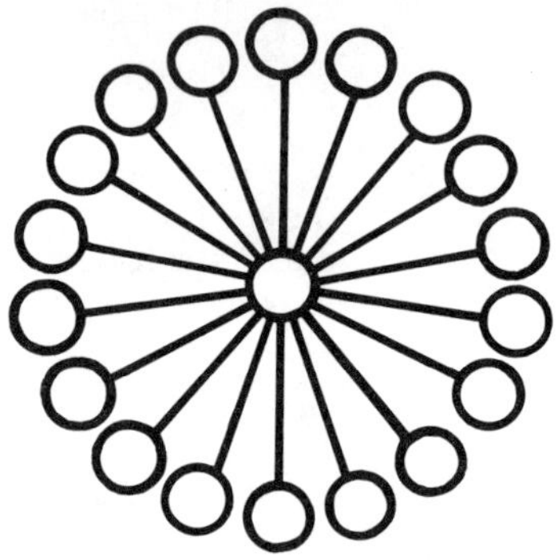

Place the numbers 1 to 19 into the 19 circles so that any three numbers in a row will give the same sum.

We are faced with two very difficult tasks: to determine the common sum for each row of spokes (three circles in a line) and then to place the 19 numbers into the correct circles. The number of possibilities for each task are so large that guess and check and other strategies seem too inefficient. Therefore, let us consider a simpler problem.

The simplest case that involves any real choice among numbers uses five circles:

Place the numbers 1 to 5 into five circles so that any three numbers in a row give the same sum.

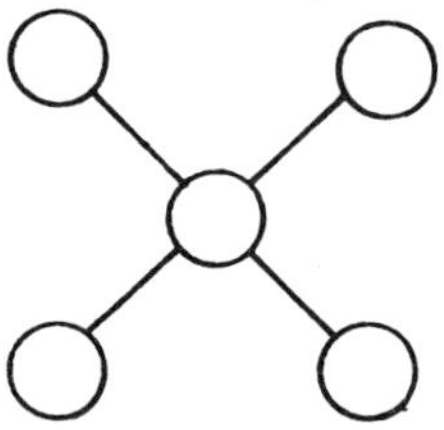

Since the number that goes in the middle circle will appear in both sums, we can simplify the problem still further by simply looking for two number pairs from 1 2 3 4 5 that give the same sum, and then placing the remaining number in the middle.

With very little effort, we can find three possibilities.

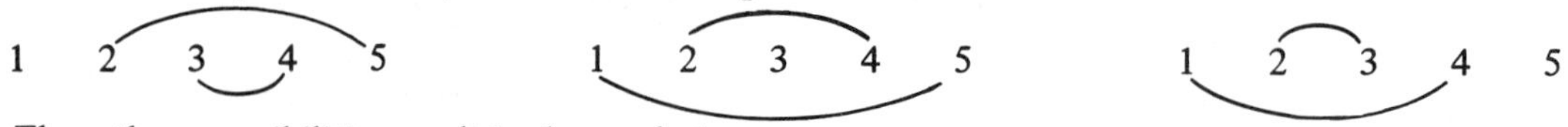

These three possibilities result in these solutions:

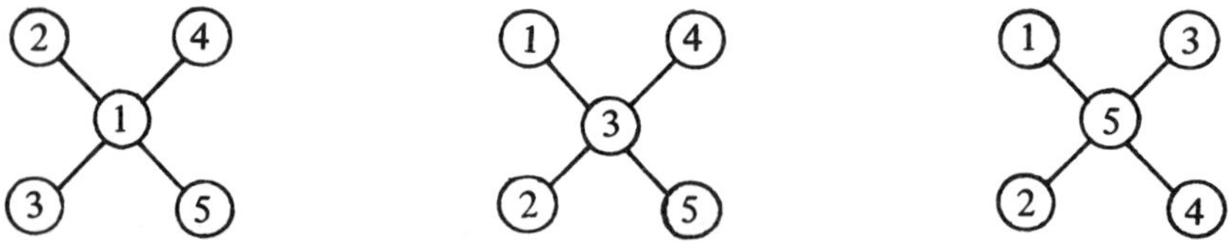

sums are 8 | sums are 9 | sums are 10

Now we need to examine our solutions for this simpler case to determine relationships that we can use in the more difficult problem. Looking at the spoke solutions, we observe that an averaging action has to occur. When a small number is placed in an outside circle, a correspondingly larger number must be placed on the opposite side of the diagram. If we look at the sequence diagrams (numbers listed in order), one number is removed, then the smallest and largest numbers are paired, and next smallest and next largest. Furthermore, we observe that our picks for the number in the middle circle were the first number of 1-5, the middle number of 1-5, and the last number of 1-5. These three selections are the only possibilities for the middle circle number.

Armed with this information, we are ready to reconsider the original problem. If we select 1 for the middle circle and pair the remaining numbers largest to smallest we have:

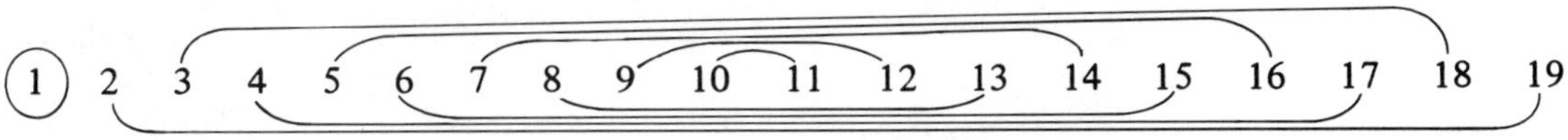

Our spoke diagram becomes

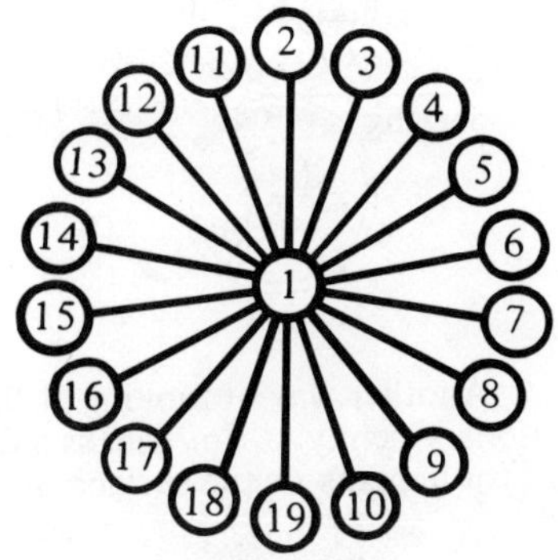

Sums of 22

By considering a simpler problem, we reduced a seemingly difficult problem to an easy task. We leave it as an exercise for the reader to find solutions using 10 (middle number of 1-19) and 19 (last number) in the center circle. (See Appendix B, page 54, for answers.)

Sometimes solving a simpler (or similar) problem may involve looking at more rather than fewer possibilities.

Grades 6 & 7 Paper Thickness

How thick is a sheet of paper? Find the answer using only a ruler as your measuring instrument.

Stop and think about it.

Have you concluded that a simpler (at least in terms of time and accuracy) problem is to find the thickness of several sheets of paper and then divide. Using a ream (500 sheets) of paper, the combined thickness is 55 mm. Therefore, one sheet of paper is 55÷500 = 0.11 mm thick!

Try solving a similar or simpler problem as a strategy for this question.

Grades 7 & 8 Penny Roll

If a penny is rolled around a second penny, starting as shown, will Lincoln's head be facing up or down when rolled halfway around? Explain.

Stop and work on the problem.

It is easy to act this problem out to establish that Lincoln's head will face upward. But why is this so?

Consider a similar problem, rolling a penny the same distance on a flat surface. What happens? How is this problem related to the given one?

Rolling a penny half its circumference on a straight surface produces the expected upside down position.

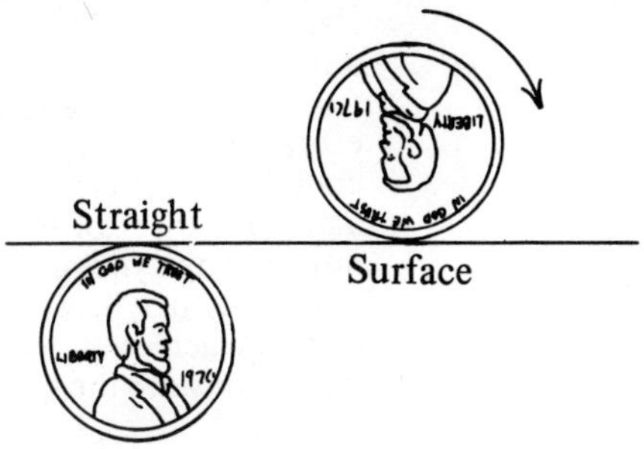

To compare this situation to rolling on a curved surface (another penny) requires wrapping our straight surface around the curved one.

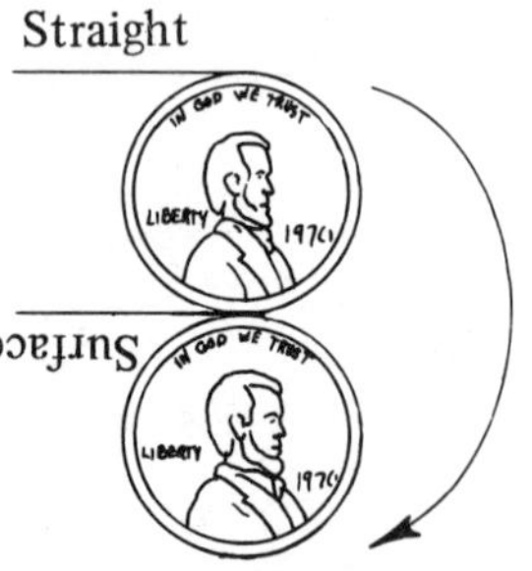

This turns the penny upside down. The two actions together make it appear heads up to us.

Another way of looking at this problem is to consider what "up" means to the surface of the stationary penny. "Up" means a direction outward from the center. A comparable situation is that for humans on the surface of the earth.

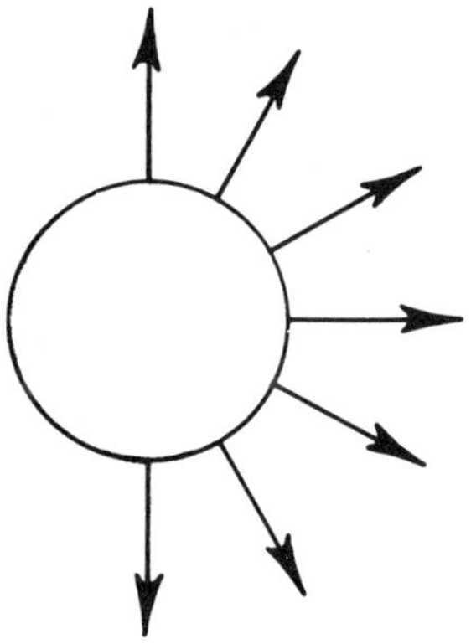

When the penny has turned half its circumference on the stationary penny's surface, its position is now upside down *relative to the rolling surface!* Turn the page around and convince yourself.

This problem may not appear to be mathematical to some readers. Whether it is or not (and we think it is) is unimportant to our discussion. It does represent a problem, and one which can be understood by application of the strategy *solve a similar problem.*

Strategy: Change Your Point of View

Various factors can make a problem difficult. Most we have no control over, but one that is within our discretionary power is the perspective we take of the problem. Upon meeting most problems, we tend to quickly adopt a particular point of view. We speedily formulate a plan of attack and then implement it to determine whether it produces a solution. If our plan is not successful, the tendency is to return to the same point of view and adopt a new plan. This may be successful. But it may also involve a circle of faulty logic based upon an incorrect or non-productive initial perspective.

The real culprit in this process is failure to examine adequately the problem initially. The better we understand the full nature of a problem, the more likely we are to choose a successful line of attack. However, it is human nature to progress rapidly through the problem identification stage. We should therefore acknowledge this human frailty and provide a means to escape from a failure cycle created by an unsuccessful initial view of a problem.

We recommend the strategy *change your point of view.* That is, cease current problem efforts, discard any previous notions about the problem, and try to redefine the problem in a completely different way. Unlike *restating the problem,* changing your point of view requires a major shifting of focus upon the problem components. Elements which were emphasized are now downplayed or perceived in a different manner. Other problem features are highlighted that previously may have been given very little consideration. We try to imagine how the problem state could be achieved in ways other than that initially conceived.

Consider the perspective that you adopt in reading the following problem.

Grades 8 & 9 Planning a Tournament

617 teams are about to begin a single elimination basketball tournament – one loss and you are out. How many games total must be played to crown a champion?

Stop and consider how you might go about the problem. Even if a specific plan does not occur to you, you will probably be able to identify a task that needs resolving in order to answer the question.

Most people who have some knowledge of tournament situations begin thinking of brackets. For example, if four teams are playing, the teams are paired in this fashion.

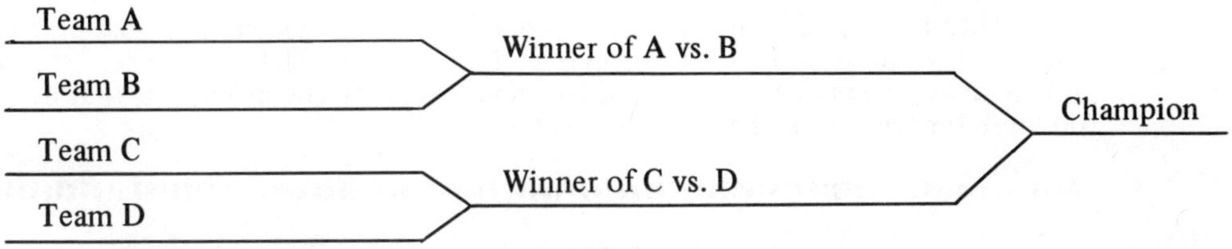

For the four team bracket above, three games must be played. However, if the number of teams playing is not a power of two, byes are necessary. That is to say, all teams will not have to play in the first round. Some teams will automatically progress to the next round while some will have to play a game to determine who goes on. This reduces the field to a power of two so that pairings will be equivalent from that point on.

For example, if six teams are to play, two teams receive byes and four teams must vie for the other two positions of round two.

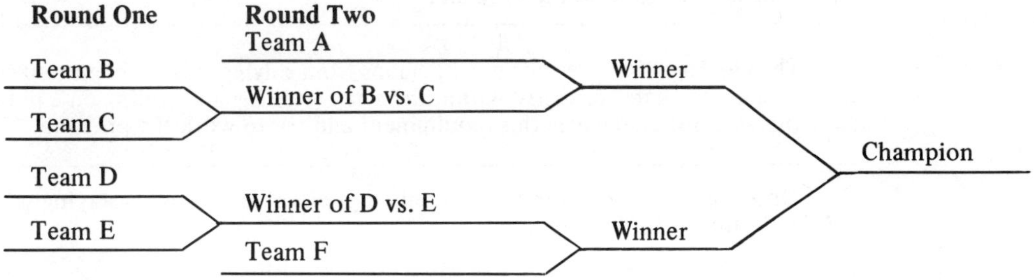

Counting, we observe that five games are necessary to determine the champion.

With so many complicating factors involved with 617 teams, it seems hopeless to find the total number of necessary games by counting. So let us return to the original problem and re-examine the perspective we have taken. Perhaps we have assumed a view that can be improved through a change in focus.

We have visualized two teams playing, the winner advancing and the loser out of the tournament. A diagram such as that above keys on what happens to the winners. Without realizing it, we have concentrated our attention upon **winners** – counting games until only one team is left which has won all of its games.

Suppose that we now focus on losers. Every time a game is played, one loser is determined. What has to happen to end the tournament? We must produce 616 teams that lose a game (the remaining team will win all of its games). Therefore, 616 games must be played, in which 616 teams will lose and be out of the tournament.

Changing our point of view made the problem much simpler.

Grades 6 & 7 The Test Track

A test track for new cars is exactly one kilometer around. For the first lap, the test driver averages 30 km/h (kilometers per hour). How fast does the car have to travel the second lap, to average 60 km/h for the two laps?

Most people have the tendency to say, "Drive the second lap at 90 km/h. The average will then be $\frac{30 + 90}{2} = 60$." We will tell you that this is not the correct answer, and advise you to change your point of view of the problem to solve it. Now stop reading and work on the problem.

Since the problem involves distances, rates, and times, we are restricted in what we may consider. The incorrect solution of the problem concentrated on rates. To change our point of view, we may consider distance or time. We select time and recall that d = r x t (distance equals rate times time).

If the car averages 30 km/h for a distance of 1 km, how much time is required?

$$1 = 30 \times t \qquad \text{so } t = \frac{1}{30} \text{ hr or 2 min}$$

If the car is to drive a distance of 2 km (including the first and second lap) at an average speed of 60 km/h, how much time will it take for 2 laps?

$$2 = 60 \times t \qquad \text{so } t = \frac{2}{60} \text{ hr or 2 min}$$

Therefore, his time for the first lap plus that for the second lap must be 2 minutes. But he has already used the 2 minutes for lap one. He has no time left, no matter how fast he might be able to drive, to complete the second lap. The answer to the problem is that he cannot average 60 km/h for two laps if the first lap speed was 30 km/h.

A simpler application of this strategy is involved in this problem.

Grades 3 & 4 Nine Dot Path

Without lifting your pencil from the paper, draw four straight line segments through the 9 dots.

Stop and try to solve the problem.

The blockage that prevents most persons from solving this problem results from their trying to keep their segments contained within the array (starting and ending on a point). If you have made this assumption, change this requirement and try to work the problem.

Once a person recognizes that nothing in the problem imposes staying within the array, the solution is usually forthcoming.

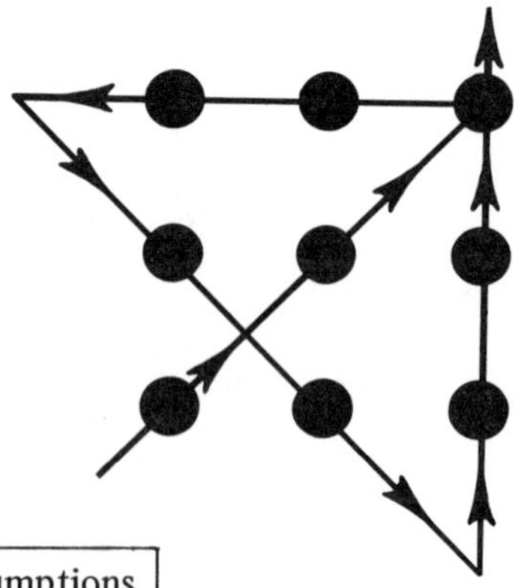

Strategy: Check for Hidden Assumptions

One reason for employing the strategy *changing your point of view* is to get out of a non-productive loop. This situation occurs because we have taken a view of the problem that presents us with obstacles too difficult to overcome (in a reasonable time period).

However, we sometimes find ourselves in a failure loop that we cannot break by changing our viewpoint. This difficulty may be the result of an incorrect inference suggested by the problem or drawn by the solver for some reason in his previous problem solving background — negative feedback, in other words. To allow for this possibility, it is wise to *check for hidden assumptions* when a problem proves particularly troublesome. This can be accomplished by asking yourself questions such as: "What **precisely** does the problem say and **not say**? What am I assuming that may not be implied or necessary? Is the result suggested in the problem (or my thinking) necessarily true? Could it be false?"

Sometimes problems are created to purposely mislead the solver, but all too frequently the solver draws the mistaken inference himself.

Grades 6 & 7 The Missing Dollar

Three men agree to share a hotel room and pay $30 when they check in. Later, the clerk finds that he should have charged them only $25. He sends the bellhop up with $5 refund for the room. But the bellhop cannot divide $5 evenly by 3, so he returns only $3 to the men and keeps $2. Therefore, each man paid only $9 as his share of the room for a total of $27. The bellhop kept the other $2 for a total of $29. What happened to the extra $1?

This kind of question represents a class of problems wherein an incorrect relationship is inferred. Can you stop and discover the hidden and false assumption?

Changing the conditions of the problem and comparing the results to those given help expose the incorrect conclusion. In the table below, we have changed the amount the clerk returns and tabulated the total room cost plus the bellhop's "tip."

Amount Clerk Returns	Amount Returned to Men	Amount Kept by Bellhop	Room Cost Per Person	Total Room Cost Plus Bellhop's "Tip"
$5	$3	$2	$9	$27 + $2 = $29
$7	$6	$1	$8	$24 + $1 = $25
$10	$9	$1	$7	$21 + $1 = $22
$17	$15	$2	$5	$15 + $2 = $17

Examining the last column, we could ask what happened to $1, $5, $8, or $13. The false inference becomes readily apparent when the conditions are changed. There is no reason the total room charge to the men plus the bellhop's "tip" should equal $30. The numbers for the problem given are such that it just happens to be close.

Trying to identify unwarranted assumptions is not always an easy task. Tackle the following activity and try to be aware of what you assume.

Any Grade Level Ski Tracks

Coming down a hill covered with snow are two ski tracks. One track goes around a tree on one side. The other track goes around the tree on the opposite side. Give 10 different physical explanations to fit these facts.

Stop and try to think of 10 explanations.

If you are average, the first two or three explanations probably came very quickly. After that you probably began to confront obstacles to your thinking. Some of the following explanations will, perhaps, expose some unwarranted assumptions you made.

1. *Man hits tree, stops, skis continue on.*
2. *Skis sent down alone.*
3. *One ski sent down twice.*
4. *One man goes on one ski twice.*
5. *Man skis to tree, detaches skis, walks around tree, refastens skis in same tracks.*
6. *Two men go down, outside marks erased.*
7. *Short tree; man goes over it.*
8. *Tree placed after tracks are made.*
9. *Pliant tree ; bends over as skier straddles.*
10. *Man goes to tree; lifted over; continues on.*
11. *Hill is part of narrow valley; man goes down on one ski, up the opposite slope, and back past tree on return trip.*
12. *Gentle slope; man lifts one ski to pass tree and replaces as he passes to show a continuous track.*
13. *Man goes through tree!!*

Challenge Problems Set IV

The following problems can be solved by an application of a strategy from this section.

A. Grades 4 & 5 — Hat Sale

Margaret opened her new hat shop Monday. In the morning, she sold her hats for $3 each, totalling $18. In the afternoon, she reduced her price to $2 each and sold three times as many. How much money did Margaret earn from her first day sale of hats?

B. Grades 5 & 6 — Four Triangles

With six sticks of equal length how can you form four equilateral (all sides equal) triangles without breaking or cutting the sticks?

C. Grades 6 & 7 — Checkerboard Squares

How many squares are there on a checkerboard? (They can be different sizes.)

D. Grades 5 & 6 — Double Trouble

A water lily doubles itself in size each day. From the time the original plant was placed in a pond until the surface was completely covered took 30 days. How long did it take for the pond to be half-covered?

E. Grades 6 & 7 — Magic Square

Fill in the following square so that all sums (rows, columns, and main diagonals) are the same, using the numbers 5-13 to fill in the square.

FINAL PROBLEM CHALLENGE TEST

You have studied 16 strategies intended to make problem solving an easier and more enjoyable activity. Thus far, you have studied the strategies in groups. However, the final measure of how good a problem solver you have become will be determined by how well you can select and use the strategies without any hints as to which may be more appropriate.

This final test will give you an indication of how far you have progressed, and perhaps, point out that continued emphasis given to problem solving prowess is still worthwhile.

There is no time limit for working on these ten problems. You may find using the strategy check list on page 45 helpful in organizing your efforts. Evaluate yourself according to the following scale.

RATE YOURSELF AS A PROBLEM SOLVER	
0 correct:	Boo! You are the kind of person who reads books by skipping to the end. Go back and work from the beginning.
1-2 correct:	Take heart. This achievement shows progress from where you started. But remember to keep flexing those strategies.
3-5 correct:	A laudatory performance. You have joined the ranks of active problem solvers who delight and succeed in solving problems everywhere.
6-8 correct:	Excellent. You have become a master problem solver and can expect to have others turn to you for expert help.
9-10 correct:	Superb! You are now officially designated a Grand Master Problem Solver and entitled to all honors and privileges resulting therefrom.

1. Grades 4 & 5 Boat Problem

Eight men and two boys want to cross a river using a small canoe. The canoe can carry two boys or one man. How many times must the canoe cross the river to get everyone to the other side?

2. Grades 5 & 6 Pizza Pieces

Fred can have any size piece of pizza he would like provided he can name the fraction of the whole pizza the piece is. What size piece(s) could you have if you were Fred?

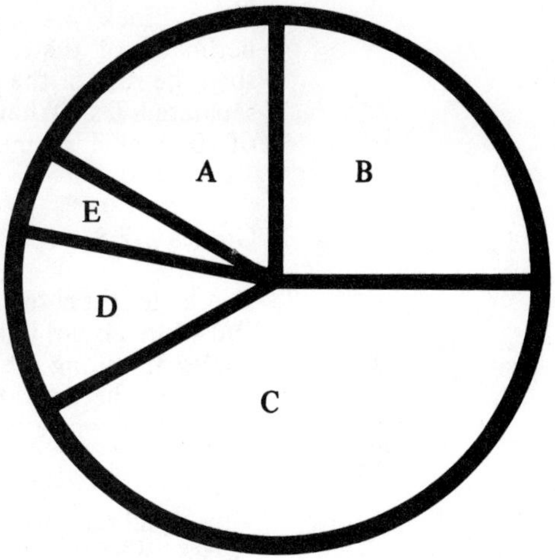

3. Grades 3 & 4 — At the Fair

Jan and Sue were throwing balls into these baskets at the fair to win a prize. A total score of exactly 34 points won the largest prize. What is the **least** number of balls needed to score exactly 34?

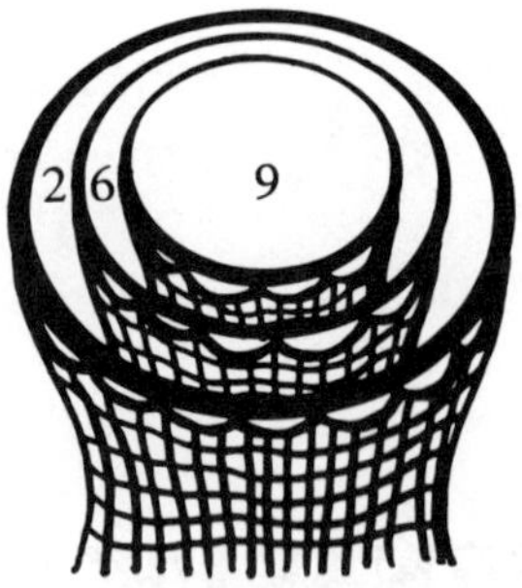

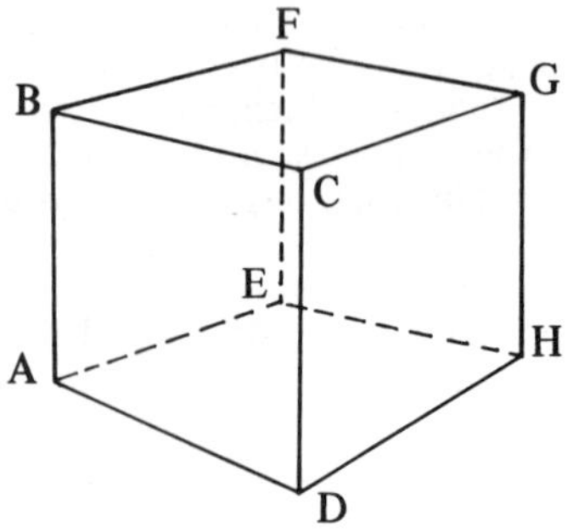

4. Grades 3 & 4 — A Worm's Trip

How many ways can Wilhelm the Woolly Worm crawl from A to G along the wire frame if he takes a 3-sided trip?

5. Grades 5 & 6 — Summer Fun

Using only the numbers 1, 2, 3, 6, 7, 9, 0 find which number goes with each letter in the addition problem to make it correct.

	S	U	N
+	F	U	N
S	W	I	M

6. Grades 8 & 9 — Train and Tunnel

A train traveling at 60 miles an hour takes 5 seconds to enter a tunnel and a further 40 seconds to pass completely through the tunnel. What is the length of the train and what is the length of the tunnel?

7. Grades 5 & 6 — What's on the Cube?

Given the desk calendar at the right, what are the remaining numbers on the dark and light cubes? Remember, all dates from 01-31 must be possible.

8. Grades 5 & 6 — Block T's

When block T's are joined, the perimeter of the new figure is less than the sum of the perimeters of the separated T's. What is the perimeter of 20 block T's joined together?

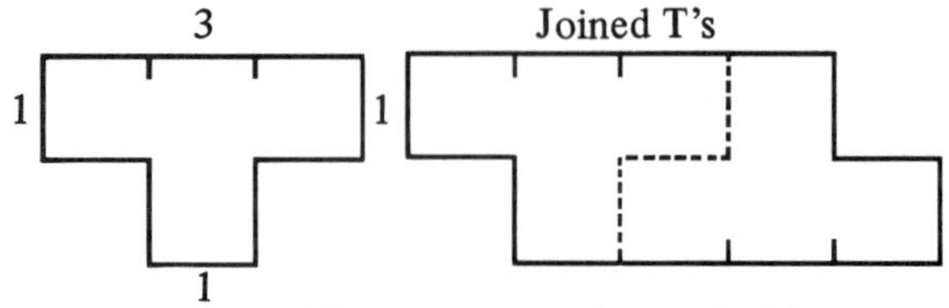

perimeter is 10

perimeter is 14

9. Grades 7 & 8 — Circle Table Mats

The table mat shown is made of black and white circles joined so that black circles are along the edge and white circles in the interior. Twenty black and sixteen white circles are used.

There are two such table mats made with equal numbers of white and black circles. What sizes are they?

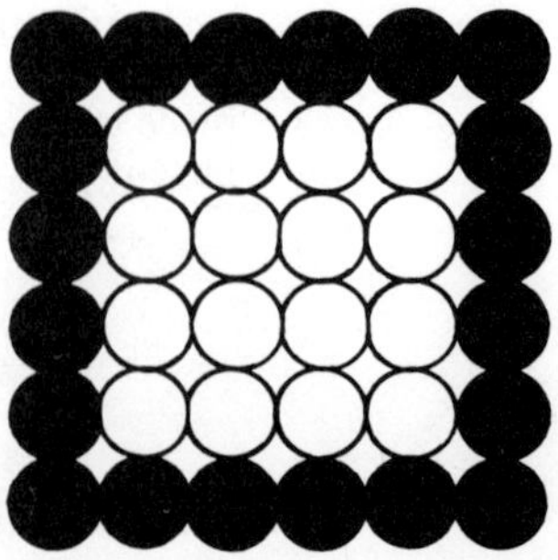

10. Grades 5 & 6 **Who Won the Tournament?**

During three successive seasons, the Boston Celtics, St. Louis Hawks, Cincinnati Royals, and New York Knicks each reached the playoffs in professional basketball. A different team won each year. But the Hawks never beat the Celtics. The Knicks lost all of their games. And the Royals never lost to the Celtics. Can you complete the championship brackets for each of the three years?

1936

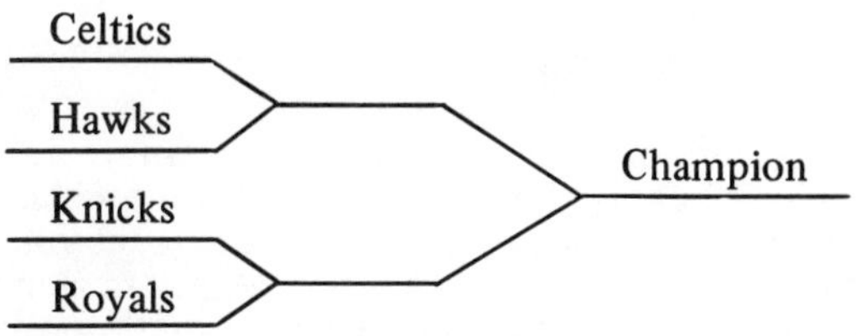

1937

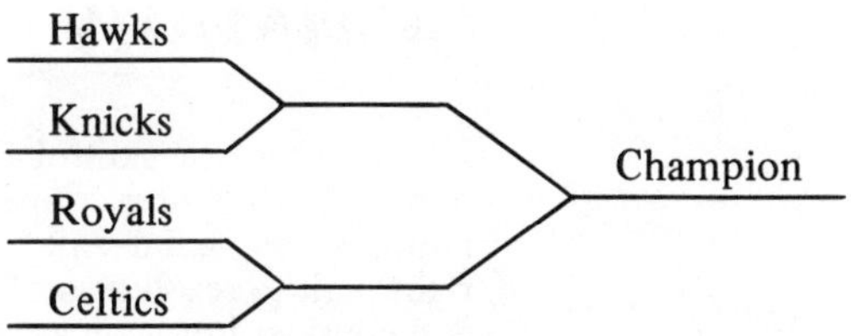

1938

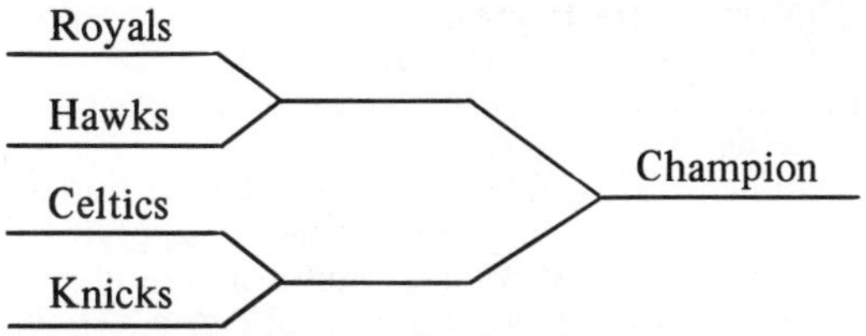

STRATEGY CHECK LIST	
Look for a pattern	___
Construct a table	___
Account for all possibilities	___
Act it out	___
Make a model	___
Guess and check	___
Work backwards	___
Make a drawing	___
Select appropriate notation	___
Restate the problem	___
Identify given, wanted, needed information	___
Write an open sentence	___
Identify a subgoal	___
Solve a simpler problem	___
Change your point of view	___
Check for hidden assumptions	___

SUMMARY

To become skillful at solving all kinds of problems, you must be aware not only of the particular attributes of specific problems but also how you interact with problems generally. This requires using good skills, perhaps without conscious consideration, that get you started on the right path to resolution of the problem. It may also entail the capability to step outside yourself and consider how you are approaching the given situation, what you are trying and not trying, why you may be unsuccessful though trying mightily, and what you have left untried that may prove to be successful.

Each of these actions or skills might fall under the heading of common sense. We have called them strategies. Some persons already use many of these techniques routinely without being aware of their use. Others use them hardly at all. Our contention is that you will be more likely to use productive thinking techniques to solve problems by (a) being aware of the techniques and (b) practicing them.

Through this booklet, you have had the opportunity to do both. Though we have used mathematical formats to give you practice applying strategies to problems, we feel confident that your general problem solving capabilities have improved also. The value of strategies is that they are content-free and they are action-oriented. They may be applied to all manner of problems. They result in outcomes – outcomes that may solve a particular situation, generate additional information about the problem, or generally point toward other things to try until the problem eventually yields.

The task of improving your problem solving abilities is a never-ending one. But it is also a pleasurable one because you are rewarded on the spot with the satisfaction and exhilaration of having mastered another problem, and in the process having added to your problem solving repertory.

As an educator, your purpose in improving your ability to handle problems is twofold: to become a better problem solver yourself for personal use and to become more proficient to teach others how to improve their abilities. As a teacher, there is a great deal to be learned by examining your own thoughts and actions while solving problems – to gain insights into how you may help others improve their thinking. However, there are many other factors which involve the learner that we have not yet considered. Moreover, there are even other strategies that are best learned, and therefore taught, in group situations even though these important looking back strategies will eventually be applied individually.

Additional considerations of the teaching and curriculum roles in developing problem solving are topics of the second part of this publication: **A Resource for Problem Solving.**

APPENDIX A: HINTS TO PROBLEMS

Set I (page 12)

A. How many school days are in two weeks? What happened to the length of recess each succeeding day?

B. If Z is the first letter, Y the second, X the third, and so on, how does the number of letters in a column compare with the column number?

C. The answer is **not** what you might think. Between what pairs of numbers will the hands overlap?

D. What is the largest odd number that could be used with 7 other numbers? Work from one solution to another by observing that a pair of odd numbers in one solution may be replaced by a different pair, whose sum is the same, to produce a new solution. The total sum will remain 20 and 8 odd numbers will still be used; i.e. replacing 1 + 7 with 3 + 5 and keeping the other 6 numbers the same will give you a new solution.

E. How much would the two methods cost for a specific number of checks, say 6 and 9? When will the second method cost less?

Set II (page 20)

A. Four removed sticks are to remove four triangles. That is an average of one triangle removed for each stick removed.

B. Does the problem prohibit you from bringing something back across the river once it is taken to the other side?

C. Area = length x width. Using the following table with different "lengths" should help you find the answer.

Length	Width (96 - 2 x length)	Area (length x width)

D. Use pennies to model the given and wanted positions of the pins. You are permitted to move three pennies to change one configuration into the other.

E. Looking at the following diagram, suppose boy 2 lost the final play. How many points did each boy have just prior to the third play?

	Play I	Play II	Play III	End
Boy 1	___	___	___	40
Boy 2	___	___	___	40
Boy 3	___	___	___	40

F. If the sheets are rolled into cylinders and fastened along an edge, they can be filled with small objects, like beans or marbles. Can more than one cylinder be formed with a single sheet?

Set III (page 32)

A. For three girls, equal shares mean thirds which you already have. Four girls mean that equal shares must be fourths. Draw the fourth lines on the diagram. Thirds and fourths are involved. What smaller fraction divides both thirds and fourths evenly?

B. Use ordered triple notation (a, b, c) where **a** represents the contents of the 8-liter beaker, **b** that of the 5-liter beaker, and **c** that of the 3-liter beaker.

C. Draw pictures to represent the problem information. How much time does it take Abe to ride one way to school?

D. To what is the difference due in the two weights if the same can is used in both weighings.

E. Can you find the number of beats in larger blocks of time than a minute, but smaller than a day?

F. Draw a picture before completing the problem.

G. If only one block is moved, how many stacks change? do not change?

H. Consider the possibilities given by each statement and selectively narrow the list with each succeeding statement.

I. Make a table and account for all possibilities.

J. Draw a picture. Consider how many tacks are required for one picture and how many more must be used as additional pictures are added.

Set IV (page 42)

A. How many hats did Margaret sell in the morning?

B. Make a model and consider simpler problems. To make one triangle requires three sticks. To add a second triangle requires two more sticks (you can use a side in common).

C. Squares can be 1 x 1, 2 x 2, 3 x 3, . . . Consider simpler problems.

How many 1 x 1 and 2 x 2 squares are there for

D. Try to change your focus of the problem. Instead of doubling repeatedly to get to the proper size, how else could this be achieved?

E. Can you complete a magic square with other numbers that might be simpler? How could you transform that square into the given one?

Final Problem Challenge Test (page 43)

1. How many crossings must occur to transport the boys? to transport a man?
2. How can you compare the sizes of pieces to each other and to the whole pizza?
3. How could you organize your guesses?
4. In how many ways could you take a shorter trip?
5. If two 3-digit numbers are added, what is the largest value S could take?
6. How do the situations look (a) before the train enters the tunnel (b) when it is inside the tunnel, and (c) as it has just exited?

7. Make a listing of dates and consider various possibilities. If you get stuck, reexamine your hypotheses and try to change your focus.

8. Consider shorter lengths of block T's first.

9. Draw a picture and consider the relationship of edge circles to interior circles.

10. Use the given to fill in as much information as possible.

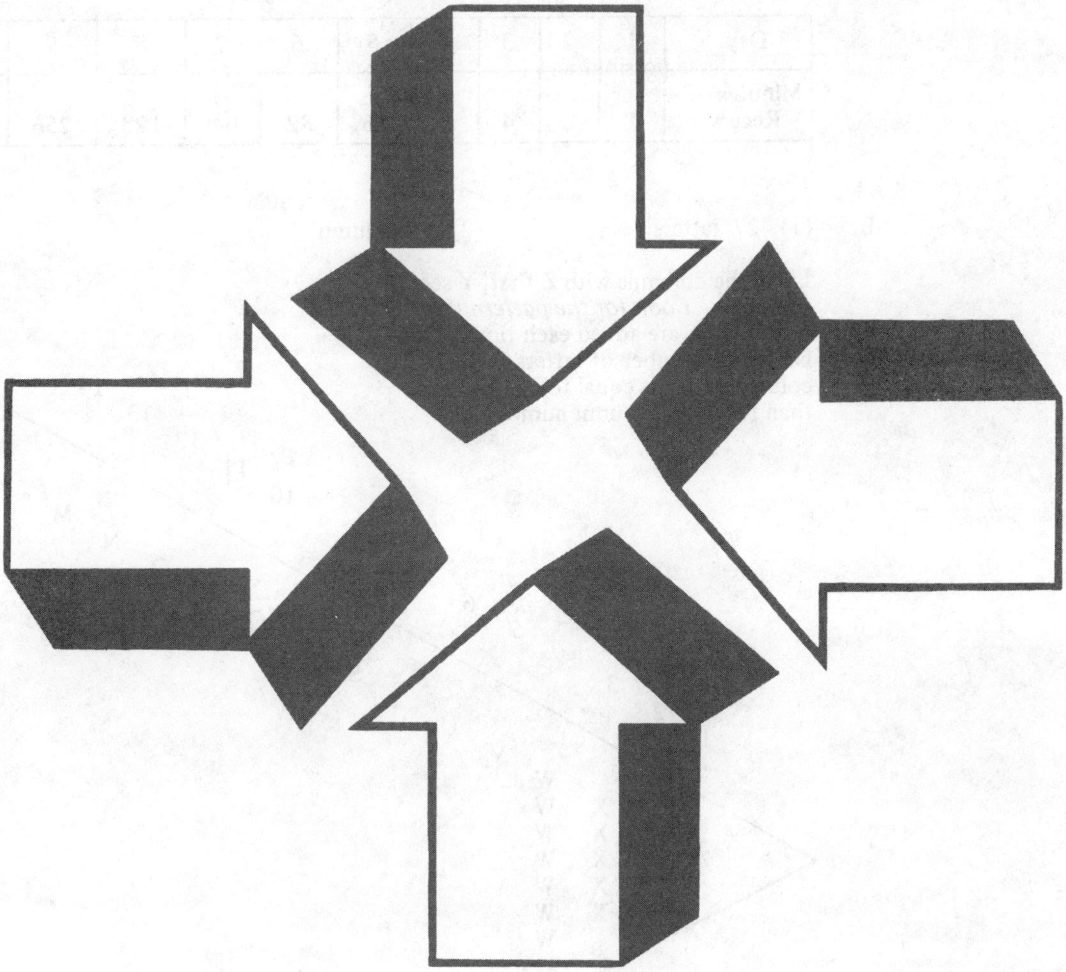

APPENDIX B: SOLUTIONS TO PROBLEMS

Set I (page 12)

A. 512 minutes or 8 hours and 32 minutes. There are 10 school days in 2 weeks, so we are looking for the length of recess on the tenth day. *Make a table.*

Day	1	2	3	4	5	6	7	8	9	10
Minutes of Recess	1	2	4	8	16	32	64	128	256	512

B. (1) 27 letters (2) J column

Label the columns with Z first, Y second, and so on. *Look for the pattern* that two more letters are added each time. There is an odd number of letters in each column which is equal to one less than twice the column number.

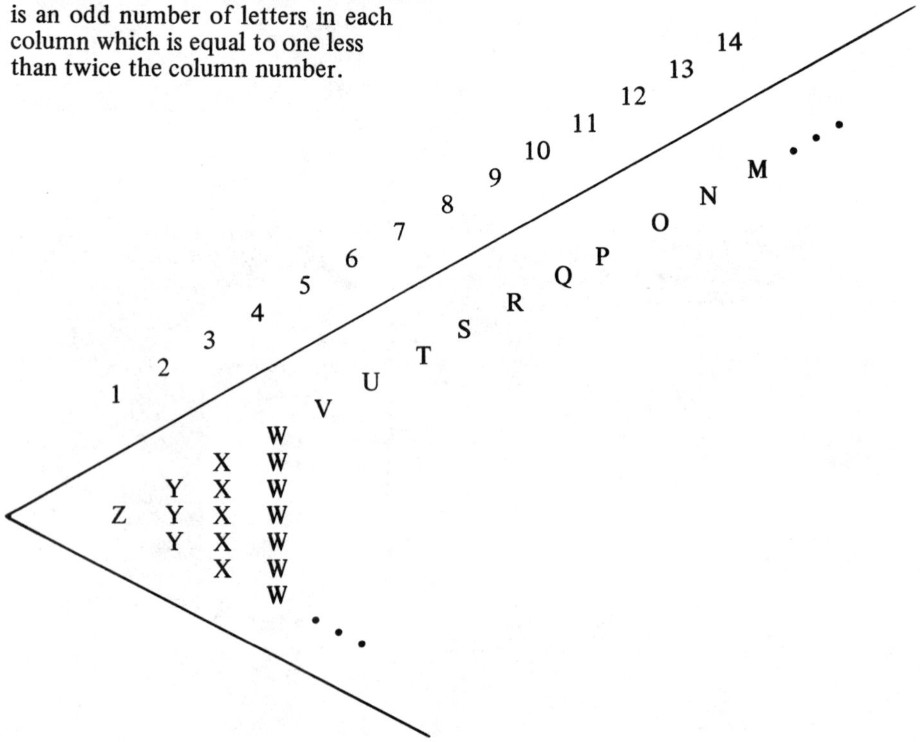

C. 11 times. *Systematically list all possibilities.* The hands will not overlap between the numerals 12 and 1, but at about 1:06. Other approximate times of overlap are 2:11, 3:16, 4:22, 5:27, 6:32, 7:38, 8:43, 9:49, 10:54, 12:00. Use your watch and try it!

D. 11 ways. *Make a table* and *systematically account for all possibilities.*

ones	threes	fives	sevens	nines	elevens	thirteens
7						1
6	1				1	
6			2			
6		1		1		
5		3				
5	1	1	1			
5	2			1		
4	3		1			
4	2	2				
3	4	1				
2	6					

E. 13 or more checks per month. By *making a table,* we can compare the two methods for different numbers of checks until the second method is the cheaper.

Number of Checks	Cost for Checks @ 10¢	Total with s.c. of 25¢	Cost for Checks @ 8¢	Total with s.c. of 50¢
6	$0.60	$0.85	$0.48	$0.98
9	$0.90	$1.15	$0.72	$1.22
11	$1.10	$1.35	$0.88	$1.38
12	$1.20	$1.45	$0.96	$1.46
* 13	$1.30	$1.55	$1.04	$1.54

Gear Train – Gear C will turn 4 full times in the same direction as gear A (clockwise).

Domino Donuts –

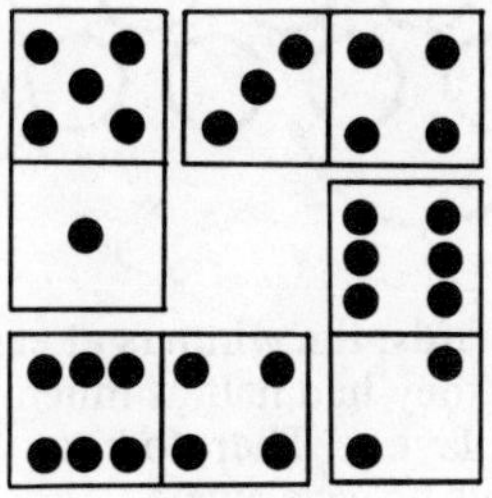

Set II (page 20)

A. Remove two sticks that remove one triangle each.
Looking at this figure, there are only two remaining sticks that will each remove a triangle.

B. Let the man (M), fox (F), goose (G), corn (C), and boat (b) be represented by letters and suppose the river is shown by a line. The following steps will result in everything crossing the river.

Step	Above the line	Below the line
Start	M F G C b	
crossing 1	F C	M G b
crossing 2	M F C b	G
crossing 3	C	M F G b
crossing 4	M G C b	F
crossing 5	G	M F C b
crossing 6	M G b	F C
crossing 7		M F G C b

C. Arbitrarily guess different lengths and fill in the table below until a maximum area is found.

Length	Width (96-2 lengths)	Area (length x width)
35 m	26 m	910 m^2
30 m	36 m	1080 m^2
25 m	46 m	1150 m^2
20 m	56 m	1120 m^2
23 m	50 m	1150 m^2
* 24 m	48 m	1152 m^2

Therefore, the maximum area occurs for a "length" of 24 m and a "width" of 48 m.

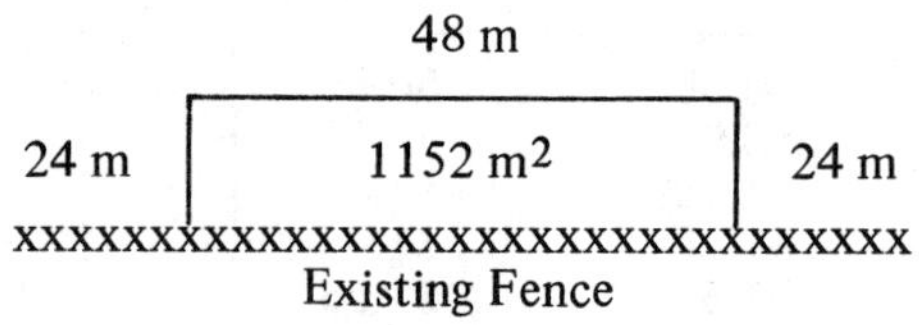

D.

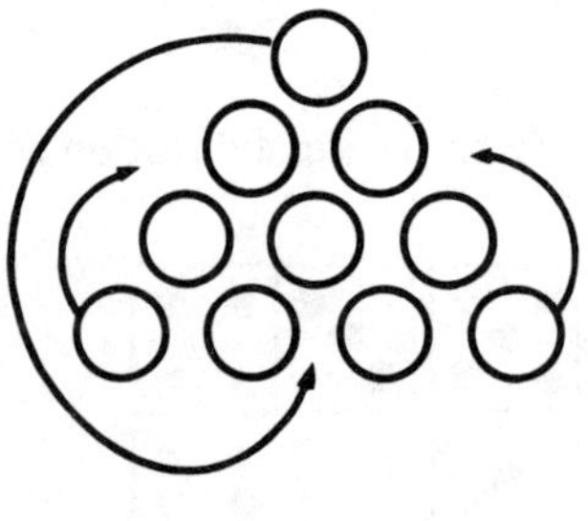

becomes

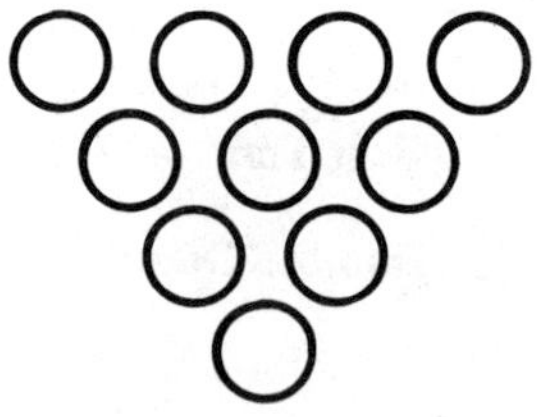

E. Working backwards, the winners at each step had their points doubled. Therefore, in the preceding play they had half as much. The loser at each step had to double the points of the other two players. Therefore, at the preceding step he had the points he has now plus the two amounts he gave away.

An asterisk indicates the loser during that play. Points are shown for the beginning of a play.

	Play I	Play II	Play III	End
Boy 1	35	70*	20	40
Boy 2	20	40	80*	40
Boy 3	65*	10	20	40

F. Either sheet will make two cylinders depending upon which way it is rolled. The dimensions of the cylinder with maximum volume (found by filling with beans) are: height – 12 cm, diameter – 9.5 cm; made from the 12 cm x 30 cm sheet.

Set III (page 32)

A. Visualize the cake cut into twelfths. Make one cut that will give her three-twelfths.

B. Use ordered triple notation (contents 8-liter beaker, contents of 5-liter beaker, contents of 3-liter beaker). The following sequence of pourings produces the required volume.

$$(8,0,0) \rightarrow (3,5,0) \rightarrow (3,2,3) \rightarrow (6,2,0) \rightarrow (6,0,2) \rightarrow (1,5,2) \rightarrow (1,4,3)$$

C. 90 minutes. A round trip both ways riding takes 30 minutes or 15 minutes riding one way. Walking, then riding, requires 1 hour or 60 minutes, of which 45 minutes must be spent walking one way. Therefore, walking both ways is double 45, or 90 minutes.

D. 15 grams. Writing two equations,

40 marbles + can = 135 grams

20 marbles + can = 75 grams

The difference in the weights, 60 grams, is due to the additional 20 marbles in the first equation. Therefore, 20 marbles weigh 60 grams. Using the second equation, 15 grams remain unaccounted for. This is the can's weight.

E. 115,200 beats. 80 beats per minute is the same as (60 x 80) beats per (60 x 1) minute [multiply both parts of the ratio by 60], or 4800 beats per hour (60 minutes). 4800 beats per hour is the same as (24 x 4800) beats per (24 x 1) hour. This is 115,200 beats per 1 day (24 hours).

F. 18 minutes

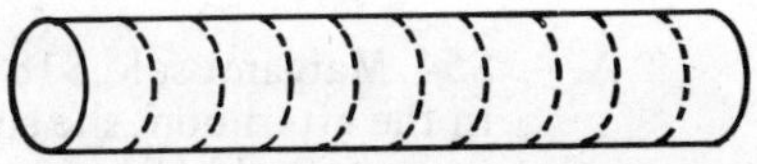

9 cuts at 2 minutes per cut is 18 minutes.

G. Move the 9 to the stack with 2, 3, 4. All sums become 18. Notice that the sum for the middle stack remained the same.

H. 480. "All three digits even but different" implies three of the digits 0, 2, 4, 6, 8 must be used and 0 not in the hundred's place. "Sum equal to 12" gives the following combination possibilities: (0, 4, 8), (2, 4, 6) in any order. "Product less than 40" rules out (2, 4, 6) leaving three-digit numbers comprised of 0, 4, 8. "Sum of hundred's plus one's digit less than ten's digit" leaves only 480 as the number since 0 cannot appear in the hundred's position.

I. 14 ways; note PAT's can only be scored after TD's.

TD	3	2	2	2	2	1	1	1	1	1				
PAT			2	1		1	1							
FG		2		1		3	1	4	2		6	4	2	
S			2	1	3	1	4		3	6		3	6	9

J. 25 thumbtacks. Arrange the pictures with edges overlapping as shown. Dots represent thumbtacks.

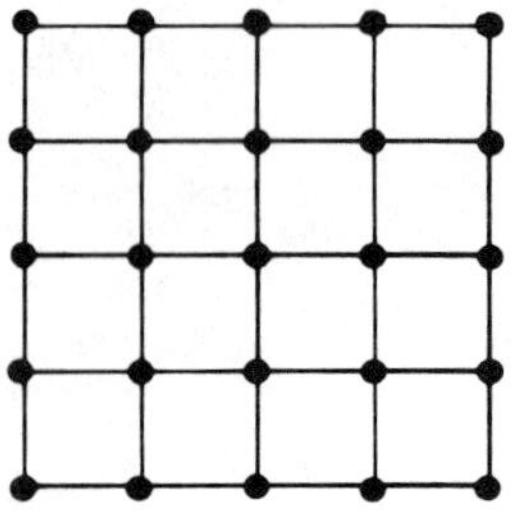

Spoke Numbers

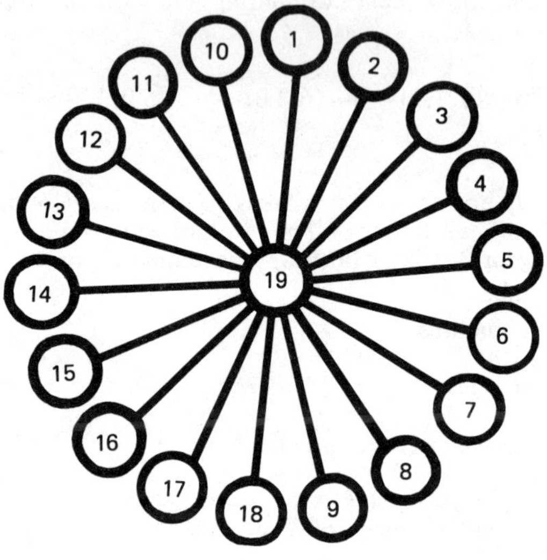

SUMS ARE 38

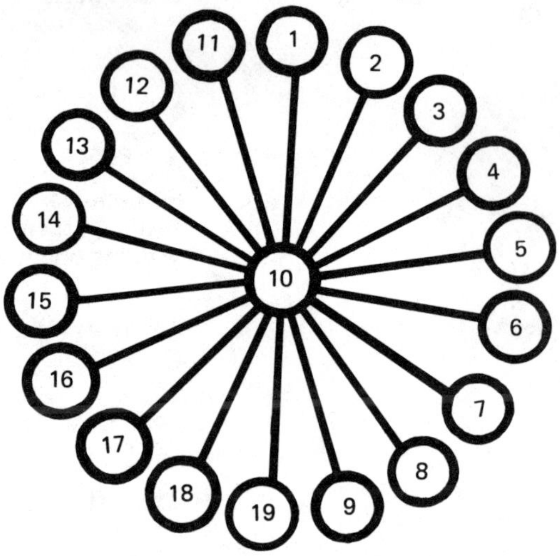

SUMS ARE 30

Set IV (page 42)

A. \$54. Margaret sold \$18 worth of hats in the morning at \$3 each. So she sold 18 ÷ 3 = 6 hats. In the afternoon, she sold three times as many or 6 x 3 = 18 hats at \$2 each. For the afternoon she sold 18 x \$2 = \$36 worth. For the day, her sales were \$18 + \$36 = \$54.

B.

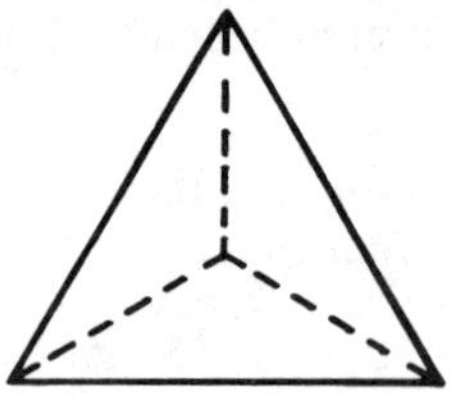

The figure (tetrahedron) is three-dimensional. In that way, the sixth stick can use two sides from existing triangles to make two new triangles.

C. 204 squares. Considering simpler cases and making a table, we have these entries.

square size	1 x 1	2 x 2	3 x 3	4 x 4	5 x 5
total number of squares	1	5	14	30	55

Look at successive differences in the total number of squares:

1 5 14 30 55

4 9 16 25

We see that each total differs from the next by successively higher squares. Subtotals represent sums of squares. By adding squares, we can find the total for an 8 x 8 square.

$$1^2 + 2^2 + 3^2 + 4^2 + 5^2 + 6^2 + 7^2 + 8^2$$

$$= 1 + 4 + 9 + 16 + 25 + 36 + 49 + 64$$

$$= 204 \text{ squares}$$

D. 29 days. Half a pond covered could be achieved starting with day 1 and doubling each day or by starting with a completely covered pond and counting back from day 30, halving each day.

E.

-3	4	-1
2	0	-2
1	-4	3

The size of the numbers and number sums makes the given problem difficult. So to simplify the problem, use smaller numbers that span a range of 9. The simplest small numbers that we might use are –4, –3, –2, –1, 0, 1, 2, 3, 4. With very little effort we can complete the square.

Then, our number range –4 to 4 differs from 5 to 13 by 9. So we add 9 to each number in the simpler problem to solve the more difficult one.

6	13	8
11	9	7
10	5	12

Final Problem Challenge Test

(page 43)

1. 33 crossings. Both boys can cross together. To transport a man requires getting the canoe back for others. To get one man across and the canoe back requires four crossings.

start
MMMMMMMM bb canoe
____

Crossing

MMMMMMMM
____
bb canoe

crossing

MMMMMMMM b canoe
____
b

crossing

MMMMMMM b
____
bM canoe

crossing

end of cycle
MMMMMMM bb canoe
____
M

Eight such cycles are required or 32 trips plus the last trip to bring the boys back across.

2. $A = \frac{1}{6}; B = \frac{1}{4}; C = \frac{5}{12}; D = \frac{1}{9}; E = \frac{1}{18}$

By tracing, we can make a model and cut out the pieces. By comparing sizes we can determine $B = \frac{1}{4}$ of the whole; $A + E + D = \frac{1}{3}$ of the whole; $2E = D$ and $D + E = A$. Since A is $\frac{1}{2}$ of $\frac{1}{3}$, $A = \frac{1}{6}$. E is $\frac{1}{3}$ of $\frac{1}{6}$ so $E = \frac{1}{18}$. $D = 2E$ so $D = \frac{1}{9}$. Then C is equal to the fraction remaining $1 - (\frac{1}{6} + \frac{1}{4} + \frac{1}{9} + \frac{1}{18})$ or $\frac{5}{12}$.

3. Six: two 9's, two 6's, and two 2's. The least number of balls is achieved by using as many large numbers as possible.

4. Six ways. ABFG; ABCG; AEFG; AEHG; ADCG; ADHG.

5. S-1, F-9, W-0, N-6, M-2, U-3, I-7.

Since two three-digit addends can never sum to more than 1998, S has to be 1. S + F has to equal 10 or 11 since S is known to be 1 which means F must equal 9.

This requires W to be 0 since 1 is already used. But then U + U (plus a possible 1 carried) must be less than 10. Looking at the one's column, N + N = M (or M + 10). Twice N has to give a result with a last digit in the list of numbers remaining. Two possibilities exist: 3 + 3 = 6 and 6 + 6 = 12. Checking the first, 2 and 7 are left for U and I; but this combination fails to satisfy the problem.

6. Train length = 440 ft; tunnel length = 3520 ft.

t = 0

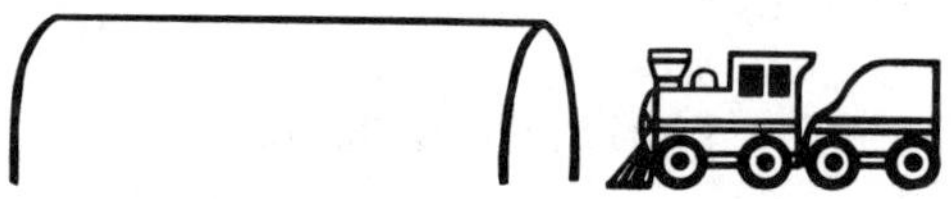

$d = r \times t$

5 seconds are required to travel the train's length at 60 mph.

$d = \frac{60 \text{ mi}}{\text{hr}} \times \frac{5}{3600} \text{ hr (5 sec)}$

$= \frac{5}{60}$ mi or 440 ft

t = 5

40 seconds are required for the caboose to travel the tunnel's length at 60 mph.

$d = \frac{60 \text{ mi}}{\text{hr}} \times \frac{40}{3600} \text{ hr (40 sec)}$

$= \frac{40}{60}$ mi or 3520 ft

t = 45

7. Dark cube 0, 1, 2, 6–9, 7, 8; light cube 0, 1, 2, 3, 4, 5.

0, 1, 2 must appear on each cube. Therefore, the light cube's faces are determined. Four numbers are needed for three faces left – an impossibility. Since the faces left and numbers cannot be changed, something else has to change. In this instance, it is our perception that one symbol can represent only one numeral. 6 and 9 are the same symbol turned upside down.

8. The perimeter is 86. Create a table to summarize the results for the first few cases.

no. of T's	1	2	3	4
perimeter	10	14	18	22

We observe that the perimeter increases by 4 with each T after the first. So the perimeter is equal to $10 + (19 \times 4) = 86$.

9. If we draw a sketch and label it as shown, then the number of circles along an edge will be given by $(l + 2) + w + (l + 2) + w = 2l + 2w + 4$. The number of circles in the interior will be given by $w \times l$. Since these two numbers must be equal, we have an equation, $wl = 2l + 2w + 4$. To solve the equation, we systematically try values for w and determine l.

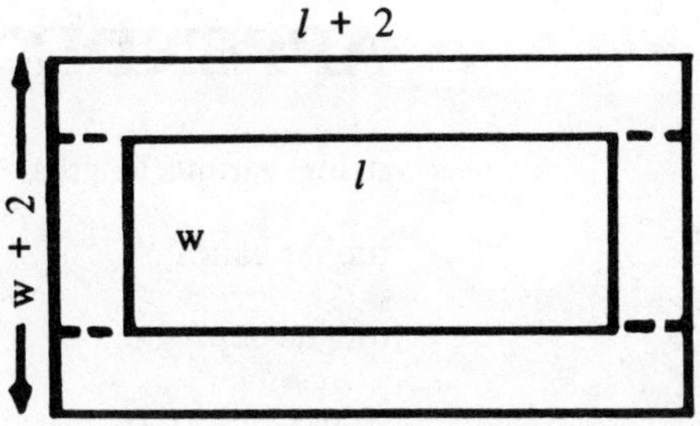

for $w = 1$	$1 \bullet l = 2l + (2 \bullet 1) + 4$;	$l = -6$	impossible
for $w = 2$	$2 \bullet l = 2l + (2 \bullet 2) + 4$;	$0 = 8$	impossible
for $w = 3$	$3 \bullet l = 2l + (2 \bullet 3) + 4$;	$l = 10$	*
for $w = 4$	$4 \bullet l = 2l + (2 \bullet 4) + 4$;	$l = 6$	*
for $w = 5$	$5 \bullet l = 2l + (2 \bullet 5) + 4$;	$l = \frac{14}{3}$	impossible

Higher values of w continue to give fractional l's.

The dimensions of the mats according to our sketch are $(l + 2)$ by $(w + 2)$. Therefore, the mats sought are 5 by 12 and 6 by 8.

10. Using guess and check, we obtain:

1936

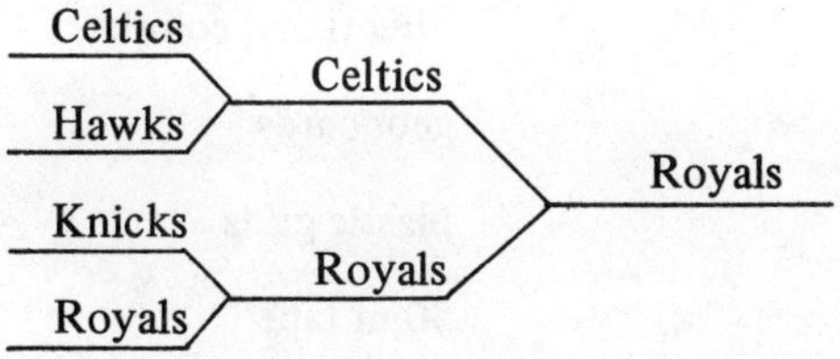

1937

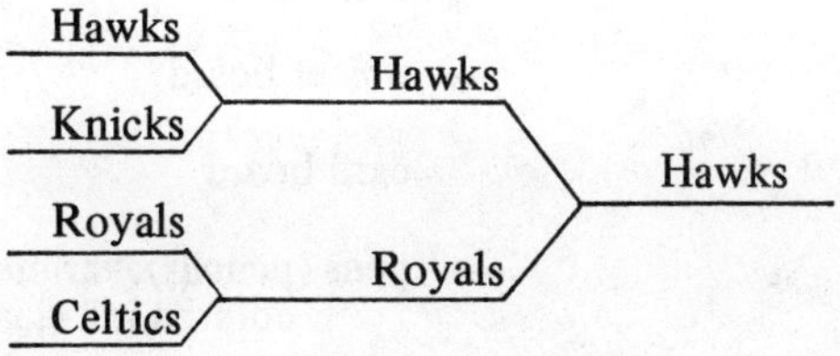

1938

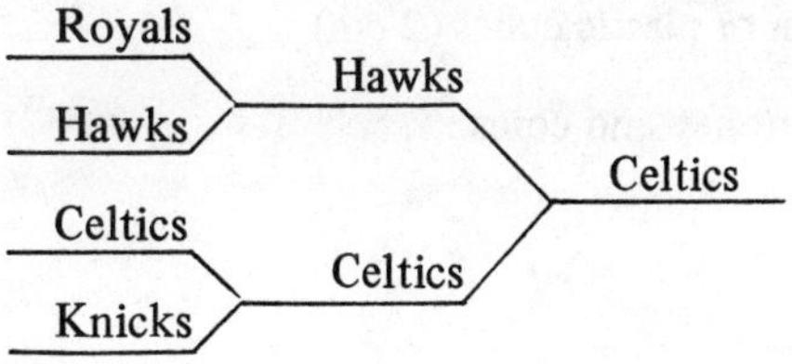

APPENDIX C: PROBLEM SOLVING MATERIALS

- string, various lengths
- rubber bands
- tongue depressors
- straws
- rulers
- scissors
- thumbtacks
- paper clips
- glue, rubber cement
- tape
- clay
- toothpicks
- scrap paper
- graph paper
- poster board
- card board
- pens (pencils), various colored ink (lead)
- geometric shapes, various colors, sizes
- wooden or plastic cubes (2 cm)
- paper money and coins
- assorted containers, various sizes and shapes
- graduated containers
- assorted objects for manipulatives
  - buttons
  - chips
  - acorns
  - bottle caps
  - cardboard squares
  - marbles
  - washers
  - miscellaneous
- sand
- saw dust
- beans
- 4-function calculator with memory
- two pan balance
- drawing compass
- directional compass
- geoboards
- plastic grids
- 50 m tape
- stop watch
- blank dice
- spinner

BIBLIOGRAPHY AND SELECTED RESOURCES

Bell, Max S. "Calculators in Secondary School Mathematics," *The Mathematics Teacher,* Vol. 71 (May 1978), pp. 405-410.

Bingham, Alma. *Improving Children's Facility in Problem Solving,* New York: Columbia University Press, 1958.

Brooke, Maxey. *Coin Games and Puzzles,* New York: Dover Publications, Inc. 1963.

Brown, Stephen, et al. *Creative Problem Solving,* Albany, New York: The University of the State of New York, The State Education Department, Bureau of Mathematics Education, and Bureau of General Education, Curriculum Development, 1978.

Brownell, William A. "Problem Solving," *The Psychology of Learning,* Chicago: Part II of the forty-first Yearbook of the National Society for the Study of Education, The National Society for the Study of Education, 1942, pp. 415-443.

Burns, Marilyn. *The Book of Think,* Boston: Little, Brown and Company, 1976.

__________. *The Good Time Math Event Book,* Palo Alto, California: Creative Publications, Inc. 1977.

__________. *The I Hate Mathematics! Book,* Boston: Little, Brown and Company, 1975.

Copeland, Richard W. *How Children Learn Mathematics: Teaching Implications of Piaget's Research,* New York: Macmillan and Company, 1974.

Doubleday, Eric. *Test Your Wits, Vol. 5,* New York: Ace Books, 1969.

Dudeney, Henry Ernest. *536 Puzzles and Curious Problems,* New York: Charles Scribner's Sons, 1967.

Frohlichstein, Jack. *Mathematical Fun, Games, and Puzzles,* New York: Dover Publications, Inc. 1962.

Gardner, Martin and Tappey, Robert. "The Paradox Box," audiovisual materials published by *Scientific American,* distributed by W. H. Freeman and Company, San Francisco: 1975.

__________. "The Aha Box," audiovisual materials published by *Scientific American,* distributed by W. H. Freeman and Company, San Francisco: 1977.

Gawronski, Jan Donnely and Coblentz, Dwight. "Calculators and the Mathematics Curriculum," *The Arithmetic Teacher,* Vol. 23 (November 1976) pp. 510-512.

Greenes, Carole, et al. *Successful Problem Solving Techniques,* Palo Alto, California: Creative Publications, 1977.

__________. *Problem Solving in the Mathematics Laboratory: How to Do It,* Boston, Massachusetts: Prindle, Weber & Schmidt, Inc. 1972.

Greeno, James G. "Solving Problems," an unpublished paper, *Agency for Instructional Television,* Bloomington, Indiana: 1977.

Harnadek, Anita. *Critical Thinking, Book One,* Troy, Michigan: Midwest Publications Co., Inc. 1976.

__________. *Mathematical Reasoning,* Troy, Michigan: Midwest Publications, Co., Inc. 1969.

Henderson, Kenneth and Pingry, Robert. "Problem-solving in Mathematics," *The Learning of Mathematics: Its Theory and Practice,* Washington, D. C.: Twenty-first Yearbook of the National Council of Teachers of Mathematics, The National Council of Teachers of Mathematics, 1953, pp. 228-270.

Hoffer, Alan. *Mathematics Resource Project Modules,* University of Oregon, (available through) Palo Alto, California: Creative Publications, Inc. 1977.

Hudgins, Bryce B. *Problem Solving in the Classroom,* New York: Macmillan Publishing Company, 1966.

Kilpatrick, Jeremy. "Problem Solving and Creative Behavior in Mathematics," *Reviews of Recent Research in Mathematics Education,* (ed), James W. Wilson and L. Ray Carry, Studies in Mathematics series, Stanford, California: School Mathematics Study Group, 1969, Vol. 19, pp. 153-187.

Kordemsky, Boris A. *The Moscow Puzzles: 359 Mathematical Recreations,* (ed), Martin Gardner, New York: Charles Scribner's Sons, 1972.

Litwiller, Bonnie H. and Duncan, David R. "Calculators and the Mathematics Curriculum," *The Mathematics Teacher,* Vol. 10 (November 1977), pp. 654-656.

Longley-Cook, L. H. *Fun with Brain Puzzlers,* Greenwich, Connecticut: Fawcett Publications, Inc. 1965.

Loyd, Sam. *Mathematical Puzzles of Sam Loyd,* (ed), Martin Gardner, New York: Dover Publications, Inc. 1959.

Maier, Norman R. F. *Problem Solving and Creativity in Individuals and Groups,* Belmont, California: Brooks-Cole, 1970.

Mott-Smith, Geoffrey. *Mathematical Puzzles for Beginners & Enthusiasts,* New York: Dover Publications, Inc. 1946.

Newell, Allan and Simon, Herbert A. *Human Problem Solving,* Englewood Cliffs, New Jersey: Prentice-Hall, 1972.

Polya, George. *How To Solve It, 2nd Edition,* Princeton, New Jersey: Princeton University Press, 1957.

__________. *Mathematical Discovery, Volume I: On Understanding, Learning, and Teaching Problem Solving,* New York: John Wiley and Sons, Inc. 1962.

Read, Ronald C. *Tangrams: 330 Puzzles,* New York: Dover Publications, Inc. 1965.

Rowe, Mary Budd. "Wait, Wait, Wait . . . ," *School Science and Mathematics,* Vol. 78 (March 1978), pp. 207-216.

Seymour, Dale and Shedd, Margaret. *Finite Differences: A Pattern-Discovery Approach to Problem Solving,* Palo Alto, California: Creative Publications, Inc. 1973.

Sharon, Sidney (ed). *Applications in School Mathematics,* Reston, Virginia: 1979 Yearbook of the National Council of Teachers of Mathematics.

Silvey, Linda. *Money Matters,* Palo Alto, California: Creative Publications, Inc. 1973.

Simon, Herbert A. "Learning with Understanding," *ERIC Information Analysis Center for Science, Mathematics, and Environmental Education,* Columbus, Ohio: 1976. (ERIC no. ED 113 206)

Sowder, Larry (ed). "Teaching Via Problem Solving," *Didactics and Mathematics: The Art and Science of Learning and Teaching Mathematics,* Palo Alto, California: Creative Publications, Inc. 1978, pp. 83-91.

Sullivan, John J. "Using Hand-held Calculators in Sixth-grade Classes," *The Arithmetic Teacher,* Vol. 23 (November 1976), pp. 551-552.

Suydam, Marilyn, et al. *Problem Solving Packet,* unpublished NSF materials, Columbus, Ohio: Ohio Regional Conferences on Mathematics Education, 1978. (ERIC no. ED 164 328)

Suydam, Marilyn and Weaver, J. Fred. "Research on Problem Solving: Implications for Elementary School Classrooms," *The Arithmetic Teacher,* Vol. 25 (November 1977), pp. 40-42.

Travers, Kenneth J., et al. *Mathematics Teaching,* New York: Harper and Row Company, 1977.

Unified Science and Mathematics For Elementary Schools (USMES), Newton, Massachusetts: Education Development Center.

Wheatley, Grayson H. "The Right Hemisphere's Role in Problem Solving," *The Arithmetic Teacher,* Vol. 25 (November 1977), pp. 36-38.

Wickelgren, Wayne A. *How to Solve Problems,* San Francisco, California: W. H. Freeman and Company, 1974.

Wilson, John W. "What Skills Build Problem-solving Power?," *The Instructor,* Vol. 76 (February 1967), pp. 79-80.

Wylie, C. R., Jr. *101 Puzzles in Thought & Logic,* New York: Dover Publications, Inc. 1957.